The Garland Library of War and Peace

The Garland Library of War and Peace

Under the General Editorship of

Blanche Wiesen Cook, *John Jay College, C.U.N.Y.*

Sandi E. Cooper, *Richmond College, C.U.N.Y.*

Charles Chatfield, *Wittenberg University*

Title No. ***210***

Volume No. ***170***

Death and Profits

A Study of the War Policies Commission

by

Seymour Waldman

with a new Introduction
for the Garland Edition by

Arthur E. Ekirch, Jr.

Garland Publishing, Inc., New York
1971

International Standard Book No. 0-8240-0336-5

Library of Congress No. LC-79-147562

Printed in the United States of America

Introduction

Death and Profits, *as its subtitle indicates, is a study of the War Policies Commission. Now little remembered, this commission was created by Congress in 1930 as a joint Congressional-Cabinet committee to investigate and report on ways "to promote peace and to equalize the burdens and to remove the profits of war." Headed by Secretary of War Patrick J. Hurley, and generally known as the War Policies Commission, there is little doubt that the commission's abbreviated title best described its major interest and function. Yet this was not exactly the Congress's intent. Disillusionment over the First World War had led to increasing demands in the 1920's for legislation to conscript wealth as well as men. The American Legion, speaking for the war veterans, called for a universal draft law, while pacifist leaders favored legislation to curb wartime profits because of their belief that the prospect of profitless war would be, in itself, a powerful deterrent to American participation in another world conflict.*

Legislation to take the profits out of war appealed originally to much the same peace sentiment in the country as the movements for disarmament and the outlawry of war. Beginning its work 2 years after the signing of the Kellog-Braind Pact in 1928, the War

Policies Commission seemed to point in the direction later taken by the Nye Munitions Investigation and the Neutrality Acts of 1935 and 1937. In the hearings before the commission, it became clear, however, that peacetime legislation to limit wartime profits might merely facilitate the conscription of both American industry and manpower. Under the War Department's Industrial Mobilization Plan, now revealed for the first time to the public, business firms were to be offered tentative contracts on a noncompetitive stand-by basis – with a guarantee of full production and satisfactory prices and profit margins in the event of war. This shift in emphasis from legislation for peace to legislation that would make war, or the preparation for war, cheaper and more efficient was disheartening to those liberals and pacifists who had favored the idea of a curb on war profits. While industrial spokesmen such as Bernard Baruch argued that a war without the lure of profits was not feasible, Norman Thomas, the Socialist leader, and other pacifists pointed out that the kind of constitutional amendment necessary for the effective conscription of wealth would probably encourage a fascist-like regimentation of every detail of American life.

To the peace organizations, whose leaders testified at the hearings in the spring of 1931, it was apparent that the War Policies Commission was concerned mainly with the problem of military preparedness. They agreed with former Congressmen Richard Bart-

holdt who told the members of the commission that the absence of State Department officials and the deference paid to War Department spokesmen at the hearings "seems to indicate that you are concerned in preparations for the eventuality of war rather than those for peace." Liberal and pacifist skepticism over the type of war profits bill due to emerge as a recommendation of the commission appeared justified when the majority submitted a report which proposed that the army be entrusted with wartime controls over American industry. Representative Ross A. Collins of Mississippi alone, in his minority report, protested against the setting of price controls by army officers. Collins also pointed out that the original purpose of the commission, to ascertain ways to take the profits out of war, could be achieved only by a constitutional amendment.

The hearings before the War Policies Commission brought out the variety of conflicting interests involved in any attempt to curb wartime profits. Although highly suspect as a means of preventing either militarism or war, the commission's proposals continued to interest Congress, and under the Nye Munitions Investigation the drive to prevent profiteering in wartime reached its peak without achieving its goal.

In the twentieth century, the idea of a war without militarism is surely a contradiction in terms. Opponents of militarism, as well as War Department strategists, understood accordingly that the mobiliza-

tion of a nation's economic resources and the conscription of its manpower had become essentials to preparedness for modern war. Diverted to such purposes, the numerous proposals to conscript or tax wealth as well as manpower could no longer be considered peace measures. The War Policies Commission, like the Nye Munitions Investigation, made it abundantly clear that, while army planners might proceed on the frank assumption of full militarist controls over the national life and economy in the event of war, peace spokesman would have to concert the means to prevent wars that could only bring more militarism in their wake. Waldman's conclusion that the War Policies Commission's failure to use its opportunities more constructively "may make the relation between death and profits uncomfortably close," has unfortunately been realized. Now almost forty years later, his warning is as appropriate to our own war-torn generation as it was to the American people in the 1930's.

Arthur A. Ekirch, Jr.
Department of History
State University of New York at Albany

Editor's Note

"Seymour Waldman had been a member of the New York *World* news staff, and from 1931 to 1933 he edited *International Disarmament Notes,* a press service to 2500 daily papers from the National Council for Prevention of War. When his book was published, therefore, Waldman was working with a skilled and vigorous antiwar lobby experienced in keeping the munitions industry and the military under close scrutiny."

DEATH and PROFITS

A STUDY OF THE WAR POLICIES COMMISSION

By

SEYMOUR WALDMAN

BREWER, WARREN & PUTNAM

NEW YORK · 1932

PREFACE

In 1918 the Armistice marked the end of that period of man's tragic helplessness, ineffable brutality, cupidity and stupidity known to history as the World War. Three years later the Treaty of Berlin signed by the United States and the new German republic officially corroborated the cessation of hostilities.

Since that time a great many people in the United States, including most of those who actually served in the War in a military capacity, those who have a mere academic or doctrinaire interest in the maintenance of peace or in preparations for war, and those persons acutely conscious of being potential machine gun and gas targets—all these, and more, have been demanding that something be done to prevent the repetition in any possible future war of the human and economic injustices which were rife in the last war. This combined protest and appeal has become known as the demand for the equalization of the burdens and the removal of the profits of war.

But the unanimity among those who enunciated this demand seemed to end with the naming of the objective. The definition and interpretation of general terms ran the gamut from distilling this demand into a law which would make it appreciably difficult for vested interests, bored and ambitious militarists, or super-patriots to plunge the nation into another war for profit or "glory," to making it relatively certain that if the Nation goes to war the accompanying misery will be shared equally by all as far as conditions permit.

Equalize the burdens! Take the profits out of war! Let all suffer alike! Draft the dollar! These were the cries. But they were neither the plaintive wails of hopeless sufferers nor the semi-apologetic appeals of diffident petitioners. They were demands by human beings filled with the fury of righteous indignation because of a strong feeling that they had been dealt with unfairly—demands which were strengthened by the vivid memory of caked, frozen blood, rigid limbs and spat steel. In short, the cries were unequivocal demands for the incorporation into law of what is generally considered simple justice.

The cause was pushed throughout the country by special articles, public lecturers, speeches and organized demonstrations. Its success was evidenced by the sympathetic respect with which the national law-makers listened to its proponents and the seriousness with which they deliberated on ways and means of doing something about it.

Finally, a joint Cabinet-Congressional commission, later baptized the War Policies Commission by the War Department, sat for several months hearing and discussing plans which would equalize the burdens and take the profits out of war, according to the economic and moral philosophy of whatever industrialist, financier, politician, or advocate (literal or otherwise) of the Pact of Paris, happened to be airing his views.

Early in the course of the hearings—I attended all of them—I realized, especially after hearing the head of the American Legion inform the Commission that a 7 per cent guarantee to capital in war-time would be satisfactory to the Legion, that either the Legion rank and file didn't want what they said they wanted or they were being betrayed by their leaders. I am inclined to believe the latter.

The hearings revealed the gigantic machine, whose intricate parts touch the entire nation, which is being constructed by the War Department and industrial magnates for use in the event of war. They revealed what a substantial provision, according to present plans, will be made in such a contingency for the godhead of our economic system, the proverbially sacrosanct *fair return on the investment.* They revealed the dangers inherent in a militarization of industry, an industrialization of the military forces, or a combination of the two.

The War Policies Commission reported to Congress on March 7, 1932, a little over a year after the first public hearing. In the main, it recommended a constitutional amendment "to eliminate all doubt concerning the extent of the power of Congress to prevent profiteering and to stabilize prices in time of war." Until that amendment is passed, the Commission recommended a program which should "be adopted as governmental policy in order effectively to minimize the profits of war and to distribute its burdens and sacrifices equitably" (sic!). This program, its sponsors announced, would seek to prevent anyone receiving a "profit due to the war" (that is, anything above the so-called normal rate) by the imposition of a war-time revenue law taxing individuals and corporations "95 per cent of all income above the previous three-year average, with proper adjustments for capital expenditures for war purposes by existing or new industries." To remove all doubt concerning its conception of distributing the war-time "burdens and sacrifices equitably," the Commission recommended "that no constitutional amendment to permit the taking of private property in time of war without compensation be considered by the Congress."

This was the answer of a commission created to consider amending the Constitution so that the human and economic burdens of war would be equalized. This was the answer of the cabinet officers, representatives and senators who composed the Commission to the demand that the "dollar" be drafted.

It startles one to know that elaborate preparations are already being made to insure profits to business during a future war when the cries of the maimed men of the last shambles are still to be heard. A government commission which limits its recommendation to legislation designed only to take war-time excess profits from business in the teeth of explicit instructions to remove the profits from war seems audacious, to say the least. This is especially true since overwhelming official data, notably war records, prove the impossibility of preventing business fraud and chicanery and the impracticability of accurately supervising corporation accounts. It would appear that there are a considerable number of American government officials and industrialists who labor under the delusion that the capacity of the people for apathetically accepting injustice is unlimited.

In the pages which follow I have attempted to show the intrinsic significance of the hearings before the War Policies Commission and also the generally unknown deep injustices which threaten the welfare of the people so that the country may, by taking action, spare itself the very dubious pleasures of hindsight wisdom which usually floods a nation after a war.

I would feel rewarded and gratified if this book should be the precursor of a much needed diagnosis of the whole problem, a study of the interlocking of our war mechanism and our economic system. It is this relationship, growing more intimate every day, which is seemingly justified by the general provisions of the National Defense Act of 1920, a law which is perhaps the most unfortunate product of the post-war hysteria of the A. Mitchell Palmer Red-baiting days. Such a work, based necessarily on a study and valuation of the reports of the Graham committee which investigated the stupendous corruption and graft rampant during the war, of the hearings of the War Policies Commission and of the 1924 committee on Universal Mobilization, is imperative if we are to be effective in preventing more national and international bloodshed. I believe that the facts contained in the pages of this book make this an obvious conclusion.

SEYMOUR WALDMAN.

WASHINGTON, D. C.
March 9, 1932.

CONTENTS

DEATH and PROFITS

A Study of the War Policies Commission

CHAPTER ONE

THE CRY FOR A "UNIVERSAL DRAFT"

-a

Since 1922 Congress has been persistently petitioned by the American Legion and other ex-soldier organizations for legislation which in the event of another war would draft dollars as well as men and equalize the burdens of war as well as remove the profits from it. The ex-service men charged that while they fought at the front for a dollar a day business men back home were making fortunes and laborers were receiving from eleven to twenty dollars a day. They said they wished to obviate a recurrence of this condition by providing for a "universal mobilization" so that if the United States should enter a war nobody would gain thereby. Those who do not fight, it was contended, should be drafted to work by the Government in the same manner as is the soldier. The "dollar" should also be drafted, and factories turned over to the Government. All this was urged as a means of minimizing the desire for war since most people would have much to lose and little, if anything, to gain by it. It was also claimed that should war be declared the Government would be in a stronger position because it would be spared such delays in industrial and military mobilization as were experienced in the World War.

The National Commander of the American Legion appointed a special Legion committee which, after conferring with the General Staff of the War Department, reported and proposed An Act to Provide Further for the National Security and Defense. This act authorized the President, when Congress should declare the existence of a national emergency, to draft all men between the ages of twenty-one and thirty or other desirable age limits without granting any exemption "on account of industrial occupation." The exemption proviso meant that a laborer who does not fight would be subject to draft just as are the soldiers. The bill dealt similarly with capital, authorizing the President to control those "material resources, industrial organizations and services" considered necessary during a national emergency. He was also authorized to stabilize the prices of any and all services and commodities required by the Government or by the civilian population.

This committee report the 1922 American Legion National Convention enthusiastically adopted. The Legion's legislative representatives in Washington were instructed to press the bill through Congress. Results came quickly. During that year, and on the same day, two resolutions were introduced in the House of Representatives. Royal C. Johnson of South Dakota, a Legionnaire, presented a bill incorporating the Legion bill word for word while John J. McSwain of South Carolina, also a Legionnaire, asked for the designation of a Congressional committee to weigh the proposal and report thereon. At that point, it seemed, the Legion hit a brick wall. The House took no action on either bill. Two years later, however, in 1924, the Legion proponents of this measure were joined by Senator and Legionnaire Arthur Capper. The Capper-Johnson Universal Draft Bill, ostensibly framed to "take the profit out of war" and to "conscript capital," proposes to make the President absolute dictator not only in war-time but when he believes war "to be imminent." In this case he is given control over all the "material resources, industrial organizations and services over which Government control is necessary to the successful termination of such emergency." The bill, which neither empowers the President to "conscript capital" nor requires him to "take the profit out of war," has never been reported out of committee in spite of strong Legion pressure.[1]

[1] The text of the Capper-Johnson Bill follows: "Be it enacted by the Senate and House of Representatives of the United States of America in Congress assembled, That in the event of war declared by Congress to exist, which in the judgment of the President demands the immediate increase of the Military Establishment, the President be, and he hereby is, authorized to draft into the service of the United States such members of the unorganized militia as he may deem necessary: Provided, That all persons drafted into service, between the ages of twenty-one and thirty, or such other limits as the President may fix, shall be drafted without exemption on account of industrial occupation.

Sec. 2. That in case of war, or when the President shall judge the same to be imminent, he is authorized and it shall be his duty when, in his opinion, such emergency requires it,—

(a) To determine and proclaim the material resources, industrial organizations and services over which Government control is necessary to the successful termination of such emergency, and such control shall be exercised by him through agencies then existing or which he may create for such purposes.

(b) To take such steps as may be necessary to stabilize prices of services and of all commodities declared to be essential, whether such services and commodities are required by the Government or by the civilian population.

These Congressional defeats served only to intensify the efforts of the Legion for a universal draft law. Agitation for its enactment became "one of the major activities of the American Legion"; a convention ordained it a "primary legislative effort." But the sharing of primacy gave way to fundamentalism. The 1928 National Convention of the American Legion decreed that the Universal Draft "should be the first order of business for the American Legion until enacted into law." Commander E. E. Spafford requested the members of the Legion to send to political oblivion those legislators who refused to support the bill.

The Legion went to the country and secured the support of both national parties.[2] The Democratic platform of 1924 said: "In the event of war in which the man power of the Nation is drafted, all other resources should likewise be drafted. This will tend to discourage war by depriving it of its profits." The plank in the Republican platform was even more explicit: "We believe that in time of war the Nation should draft for its defense not only its citizens but also every resource which may contribute to success. The country demands that should the United States ever again be called upon to defend itself by arms the President be empowered to draft such material resources and such services as may be required, and to stabilize the prices of services and essential commodities, whether utilized in actual warfare or private activity." They even received the accolade

[2] It is generally conceded that only about 25 per cent of the nation's World War veterans belong to the American Legion. But because of its high degree of organization the public very often forgets that its voice is not that of the body of the Nation's former soldiers.

of presidential endorsement from former President Coolidge in his speech before a Legion assemblage. Both major parties, in their 1928 platforms, again embodied favorable references to the movement for a universal draft. In the same year the tenth convention of the Legion called upon every member, Post and Department "to bend every effort toward disseminating information thereon, arousing and sustaining interest therein, and crystallizing public opinion for this measure to the end that we may safeguard our country through the passage of this admirable peace-promoting and far-reaching piece of legislation."

It was during this period that one of the avowed purposes of "universal mobilization" suffered a complete metamorphosis. "Universal mobilization" entered the political arena as an apparent peace measure, only to become an unequivocal war measure. In 1924 it was referred to by the sixth National Conference of the American Legion as "legislation which the Legion believes will help insure our country against war and provide that in any future emergency there shall be no more slackers or profiteers and that we shall have in the future equal service for all and special profit for none." The American Legion, a few years later, called the same legislative project a law "that will enable the country to quickly mobilize all its resources in case of war, so that in such event there shall be no profit, privilege or favoritism to any person or class, and that the obligation of defending our nation's ideals and sovereignty be borne equally by every American." Somewhere between these two pronouncements the peace idea evaporated.

Finally, the demand for a universal draft statute induced the Seventy-first Congress to create a joint Cabinet-Congressional commission under a resolution entitled "To promote peace and to equalize the burdens and to minimize the profits of war." It was composed of the Secretary of War, Patrick J. Hurley, Chairman; Charles F. Adams, Secretary of the Navy; Arthur M. Hyde, Secretary of Agriculture; Robert P. Lamont, Secretary of Commerce; William N. Doak, Secretary of Labor; Attorney-General William DeWitt Mitchell; Senators David A. Reed of Pennsylvania, Vice-Chairman; Arthur H. Vandenberg of Michigan, Joseph T. Robinson of Arkansas, Claude A. Swanson of Virginia; Representatives Lindley H. Hadley of Washington, Secretary; William P. Holaday of Illinois, Ross A. Collins of Mississippi, and John J. McSwain of South Carolina; Executive Secretary of the Commission, Robert H. Montgomery. Congress, on June 27, 1930, directed this group "to study and consider amending the Constitution of the United States to provide that private property may be taken by Congress for public use during war" and to ponder "methods of equalizing the burdens and to remove the profits of war, together with a study of policies to be pursued in event of war." [3] The Commis-

[3] JOINT RESOLUTION To promote peace and to equalize the burdens and to minimize the profits of war

Resolved by the Senate and House of Representatives of the United States of America in Congress Assembled, That a commission is hereby created to study and consider amending the Constitution of the United States to provide that private property may be taken by Congress for public use during war and methods of equalizing the burdens and to remove the profits of war, together with a study of policies to be pursued sion was categorically prohibited not only from reporting upon but even from considering "the conscription of labor. . . ."

Public hearings began on March 5, 1931, and, with two or three intermittent adjournments, ended on May 22, 1931. Unfortunately, hearings which were generally expected to afford an opportunity for discussion of the entire resolution were seized upon by the War Department and utilized at every opportunity for provocative discussions of war policies, such as the drafting of 4,000,000 men in war-time, at the expense of the other sections of the resolution. This effort was even carried to the point of changing what was formerly known as a "universal mobilization" commission for the consideration of industrial mobilization by the War Department to a "war policies" commission. Early in the course of the hearings, the War Department, in its letters to members of the Commission, took pains to print "War Policies Commission" on the stationery and to have it generally understood that this Commission was such a body. It was so identified in the press of the entire world. In fact, at the top of the first page of the printed Hearings there is the title: "War Policies Commission." Thus war and the consideration of means of carrying it on dominated the discussions of a commission whose first purpose was stated to be the promotion of peace.

in event of war. The commission shall report definite recommendations to the President of the United States . . . and to report if, in their opinion, any constitutional amendment be necessary to accomplish the purposes desired: *Provided,* That said commission shall not consider and shall not report upon the conscription of labor . . . (Public Resolution—No. 98—71st Congress, H. J. Res. 251.)

It is needless to point out that any detailed discussion of "war policies"—futile from the military angle because of the necessity for improvisation[4] in waging war—is dangerous in a period of economic distress in that it obstructs, by the stimulation of a war psychology, the efforts being made to bring about world political and economic recovery. In addition, it nourishes a hyper-sensitive nationalism which plays into the hands of those vicious business elements whose powers the resolution was designed to control.

[4] "Modern war is essentially and inevitably a process of improvisation, particularly if it lasts any length of time."—Newton D. Baker, in the hearings before the commission appointed under public resolution No. 98, 71st Cong., 2nd Ses., H. J. Res. 251 (hereafter cited as War Policies Commission Hearings), page 122.

CHAPTER TWO

PROFITEERING, THE FIFTH AMENDMENT AND "NORMAL" PROFITS

According to abstract justice a mechanic should be conscripted in war-time just as a storekeeper, or a house ought to be. But political expediency is the enemy of abstractions, especially those on justice. As already pointed out, Congress, through pressure exerted by certain divisions of organized labor, prohibited not only a report upon the conscription of labor but even the consideration of such conscription. In other words, those representatives of labor groups who interested themselves in formulating the labor proscription of the resolution were skeptical of the literal success of the so-called "universal draft" legislation—intended to conscript capital as well as men—under the present economic order. It is also conceivable that organized labor regarded this "universal draft" as a weapon which certain antagonistic forces might employ for the purpose of destroying trade unionism in this country.

If it were possible to conscript capital as well as labor, said Arthur J. Lovell, Vice-President of the Brotherhood of Locomotive Firemen and Enginemen, before the Commission,

> we would have been for such legislation; but we did not believe that could be done, having regard to the Constitution of

the United States, which provides, among other things, that property may not be taken without due process of law.

Nevertheless, he announced that there was "no doubt" in his mind that the War Department "can conscript labor."

Mr. Collins—. . . . So if the War Department's mobilization plans deal directly or indirectly with the allocation of labor or the fixing of the prices of labor, or the registration of labor, then you are opposed to them?

Mr. Lovell—Yes. There is no doubt in my mind that they can conscript labor.

Mr. Collins—Oh, there is not any doubt about that; they can conscript labor now.

Mr. Lovell—Yes.

Mr. Collins—And everybody knows that and that is one reason a great many people are not in favor of amending the Constitution, because already, under existing law, they can do just exactly what they have in their minds to do, in the event of war.

Mr. Lovell—And what has always been done, Mr. Congressman.

Mr. Collins—And under existing law and the Constitution, profits will be made or can be made in the case of war, just as they were made in the last war and that suits a certain class of folks, too. Now then, Mr. Baruch, in his testimony, made this very sensible statement, or at least I think it is sensible: "We must neither militarize industry, nor industrialize the Army." What do you think about that statement?

Mr. Lovell—I think I could go along with that fine, if that was all there was to it.

Mr. Collins—That is all.[5]

Whether the War Department can or cannot conscript labor, it would seem that Mr. Lovell's interpretation of the

[5] *Ibid.*, page 272.

constitutional provision of the resolution is not well founded in the light of the specific words of the resolution ordering the Commission to consider amending the Constitution so that private property could be taken by Congress for public use during war. Why, therefore, did he and his organization help to prevent consideration of the drafting of labor—something they believed and stated could already be accomplished?

In justice to the Firemen and Enginemen it must be admitted that their skepticism was well founded and that they had some reason for demanding their own exemption—even if only a fictional one. They simply discounted any serious consideration of amending or repealing the Fifth Amendment—a sacred cow of the Constitution—so that private property would suffer any of the pangs of conscription. It is plausible that they considered the actuality of conscription of labor in war-time bad enough without cooperating to make peace-time preparation for it a settled policy.

On this point the hearings bear out Labor's political shrewdness. It was obvious from the beginning that the overwhelming majority of the Commission had no intention of recommending to the President any form of conscription of capital in war-time, much less a procedure which would necessarily repeal the "just compensation" clause of the Fifth Amendment. Witness the following constructions of this clause:

Senator Swanson—I think the Government ought to take all the property it needs at a fair price; all I am apprehensive about is having all of the property hung up during the duration of the war, so that nobody can sell, buy, or trade in it until the war was over, and then to return it.[6]

* * * * *

Mr. McSwain—I wish to ask Colonel Robbins[7] to help us clarify some ideas of definition. Colonel, when you speak here in general terms of this resolution and various resolutions of conventions of the American Legion, about taking the profits out of war, I do not understand it is conceived by any real thinking legionnaire that we should prevent anybody from making normal peace-time profit, but that this move is to take war profits out of war?

Colonel Robbins—Quite right.

Mr. McSwain—That is, to take very excessive and unusual profits that would arise from inflation and to keep the rises in prices, which we ordinarily describe as profiteering, out of war?

Colonel Robbins—That is right.

Mr. McSwain—Whereby many thousands made many millions?

Colonel Robbins—Right.[8]

* * * * *

Mr. Hadley—The resolution dealing with the primary subject refers to it as "methods of equalizing the burdens and to remove the profits of war." In your testimony, when speaking of the profits of war, I assume you had in mind the profits which arise by reason of the war in excess of the ordinary and normal profits which would be otherwise realized. Is it your understanding that when we speak of taking the profits out

[6] *Ibid.*, page 110.

[7] Chairman of the National Defense Committee of the American Legion, President of the Cedar Rapids Life Insurance Company and former Assistant Secretary of War.

[8] War Policies Commission Hearings, page 257.

of war we are speaking strictly of war profits above the level of the normal profits?

Mr. Green [9]—That is my understanding. As I stated, a war creates an emergency and upsets the whole economic order—and, as a result, prices ascend, ascend, and ascend.

Mr. Hadley—That is my understanding too; but I wanted to see if our minds were working on the same basis.[10]

An Old Bogey

The big industrialists' conception of equalizing the burdens and removing the profits of war is reflected in the testimony of Mr. Walter S. Gifford,[11] President of the American Telephone and Telegraph Company, who stated that he recognized "the necessity for reasonable profits in production."

"Even during a war?" asked Senator Joseph Robinson of Arkansas.

Mr. Gifford—Yes, sir. I think we must upset the normal industrial organization as little as possible, bearing in mind all the time what we are trying to do is to win the war, primarily, and, secondarily, to win it with as little unequal distribution of the hardships as possible.[12]

The fear of "upsetting industry" is an old bogey. It first came into prominence thirteen years ago during the Senate's cross-examination of Major General George O. Squier,

[9] President of the American Federation of Labor.

[10] War Policies Commission Hearings, page 277.

[11] Mr. Gifford served as director of the Council of National Defense from December 1916 to November 1918.

[12] War Policies Commission Hearings, page 783.

Chief of the Signal Corps. The General, who was in charge of providing adequate organization for aircraft production and who was held to be incompetent by the then former Supreme Court Justice Charles Evans Hughes in his special aircraft investigation report to President Wilson, informed the Senate Military Committee:

> I think we shipped no training planes to France at all. It is looming on the horizon that we may be producing more than we can get across and thereby be upsetting industry.[13]

The House of Representatives Select Committee on Expenditures in the War Department, headed by Mr. Graham[14] of Illinois, which in 1921 reported the results of its investigation of the widespread profiteering and corruption in War Department expenditures, however, voiced another view of "upsetting industry." In its report, of which not one of the important statements was disproved by the name-calling minority report, it said:

> UPSETTING INDUSTRY
>
> Gen. Squier's statement before the Senate Military Committee was made shortly before Gen. Pershing cabled to him that 700 flying cadets had been from three to five months delayed in their training because of absence of planes.
>
> While Gen. Pershing, Gen. Mitchell, Maj. Foulois, and others in France were frantically calling for planes with which to train and fight, Gen. Squier was calmly studying "the horizon" to discover whether we should "upset industry."

[13] Graham committee report on "Expenditures in the War Department —Aviation," 66th Cong., 2nd Ses., Report No. 637, page 16.

[14] Now presiding judge of the United States Court of Customs and Patent Appeals.

"Upsetting industry" has been a besetting fear with the War Department, which made eight hours a day's work for soldiers on the coast. It has salvaged airplanes, copper, trucks, and all other properties, including foodstuffs in a manner not to upset industry. It has frequently sold back for a song articles produced under Government contract, to the original producers in order not to "upset industry." Airplanes costing the Government $20,000,000 were resold to the Curtiss factory for $2,700,000, or about 13 per cent of cost. Thousands of American aviators were compelled to buy at full price from the Curtiss Co. if they wanted these machines.[15]

On the constitutional aspect of the problem Mr. Gifford again based his reasoning on his inability to reconcile the taking of all profits with the winning of a war:

Mr. Collins—Would you be willing to have Congress pass a constitutional amendment, to be submitted to the States, which would provide that the Federal Government could take the use of private property without compensation?

Mr. Gifford—No, I should not, because I think, again, it would not be aiding in the winning of a war, if we were in one.[16]

The desire to preserve the Fifth Amendment was expressed by other witnesses, nearly all of whom were members of various Government boards just before or during the World War and who are at the present time connected with important commercial, financial or industrial enterprises. They might have been expected, therefore, not to disapprove of their own record for two reasons. First, they certainly would not parade their own short-comings before

[15] *Ibid.*, page 16.
[16] War Policies Commission Hearings, page 786.

a government commission even if they believed in the existence of such defects. Secondly, in the event of war during their lives, they will be in a position to assume even more important powers than those they exercised during the World War.

"Reasonable" Patriotism

In brief, the powerful industrialists and financiers were willing to lend their property to the Government on the outbreak of war upon "reasonable" terms. It is indisputable, nevertheless, that their conception of patriotism implies a recognition of the supremacy of private property over life and an opposition to an unconditional surrender of property to the Government—something they would be forced to do were the Fifth Amendment repealed or modified—thereby proclaiming that property is more sacred than human life. And as long as the due process clause of this amendment is not modified or repealed the Federal Government cannot take their property even in war-time without paying them "just compensation." Emphatically, they are not willing to surrender their possessions as the conscript is forced to surrender his body, all the prating about the logical impossibility of reconciling the loss of life with the loss of property to the contrary notwithstanding.

It would seem, however, that since Congress under the Fifth Amendment may now take private property for public use during war provided "just compensation" is given, the resolution could only imply the taking of private property in time of war without or with something less than what the courts, with unintentional irony, have termed "just compensation."[17] And furthermore, since the resolution specifically mentions "amending the Constitution" it would seem that Congress addressed itself to the Fifth Amendment. Nevertheless, the kind of "conscription of wealth" envisaged by most of the Commission was made quite clear when witnesses were given to understand that what the Commission was considering was the elimination of excess profits or war profits, that is, those profits above the usual peace-time ones.

Even Bernard M. Baruch, former Chairman of the War Industries Board, whose pamphlet "Taking the Profit Out of War"[18] proposed a freezing of prices by presidential ukase at a "normal level" on the declaration of war—even he advocated no substantial financial sacrifice on the part of capital but "war profits at a lower rate than peace profits."[19] In addition, Mr. Baruch failed either to realize

[17] The United States Supreme Court (280 U. S. Reports 234) held a return of less than 7.44%, the rate sought by the utility, confiscatory. Justices Brandeis and Stone dissented. The rate fixed by the state commission in this case was 6.26% upon the assumed value. The United Railways included the sum of $5,000,000 in its total valuation under the head "easements"; these "easements" were the privileges gratuitously given to the railways by county and city franchises to operate on the public highways.

[18] Mr. Baruch read this pamphlet to the War Policies Commission. The principle of the proposal to fix prices was originally stated by the Graham committee in the recommendations of its report on "Expenditures in the War Department—Camps," 66th Cong., 2nd Ses., Report No. 816, pages 145–46.

[19] Mr. Baruch's view is still fundamentally similar to that which he expressed eight years ago, in spite of the explicit instructions in the resolution to consider amending the Constitution so that profit could be elimi-

or to mention that a freezing of prices, aside from certain administrative, constitutional and economic objections, would not prevent the making of huge profits in such indispensable industries as those concerned with the manufacture of chemicals, munitions and armament since the tremendously multiplied volume brought on by war needs would result in great profits even at one-tenth the normal peace-time rate. Also, to expect those industrial or commercial powers, struggling for control of oil fields in the East or trade in the West, to equalize the burdens in the very war precipitated by them, directly or indirectly, strikes one as fatuous. And from the humanitarian viewpoint, Mr. Baruch, it seems, failed to realize that just what return capital will receive in the event of a war is entirely irrelevant to the poor devil who must face a vesicant gas or play host to a furious bullet. Nevertheless, Mr. Baruch considers that his plan "would go very far toward keeping the peace of the world. . . ."

The General Recommends 6 Per Cent

When one remembers that Major General Douglas MacArthur, Chief of Staff of the United States Army, in a prepared statement which he read to the Commission, proposed to Congress that industry be guaranteed a 6 per cent profit, the danger to the public interest from Mr. Baruch's

nated in war-time. In the January, 1926, *Atlantic Monthly* he wrote: "'Taking the profit out of war' is not synonymous with 'conscription of wealth,' as it is sometimes regarded. The latter is a theoretical project, prohibited by our Constitution, contrary to the spirit of our social and political institutions, and impossible in practice."

plan is apparent. It is even more than apparent when one recalls that, according to General MacArthur, "the vitally essential list" of materials necessary to the War Department's plan for industrial mobilization "now includes about 4,000 articles complete for issue."

From the standpoint of conscripting wealth and property in war-time, the War Department would be about as effective in "taking the profit out of war" as Mr. Baruch.

Mr. Collins—Suppose you were dealing with the head of the United States Steel Corporation on the price of products of that corporation. Under this plan of yours, how would you arrive at the price to be paid?

General MacArthur—By a coordinated agreement, under the set-up that we have outlined.

Mr. Collins—You called it negotiations.

General MacArthur—Yes.

Mr. Collins—Then, in negotiating that agreement, you state also, if I understood you correctly, you would undertake to pay them a profit of 6 per cent.

General MacArthur—Yes; that is correct.

Mr. Collins—A profit of 6 per cent.

General MacArthur—That is correct.

Mr. Collins—On what it is claimed is the investment.

General MacArthur—That is correct.

Mr. Collins—And you would do the same way with every other concern?

General MacArthur—Yes.[20]

In short, the acceptance of the War Department proposal to guarantee a profit of 6 per cent to industry would place a premium on the institution of war, especially in periods

20 War Policies Commission Hearings, page 382.

of economic depression, and would merely provide certain vested interests with another incentive for war.

The Legion Takes the Stand

The pronouncement of the American Legion head was a complete surprise. Until the War Policies Commission held its hearings nearly all of its members and the general public believed that what the American Legion meant by "universal draft" was as drastic a war-time conscription of wealth as of life.

In 1924 Mr. John Thomas Taylor, Vice-President of the National Legislative Committee of the American Legion, had presented Colonel John D. Markey of Maryland as the Legion's spokesman to the Committee on Military Affairs of the House of Representatives, which was holding hearings on "universal mobilization for war purposes." Mr. Taylor told the House committee that Colonel Markey was chairman of the Legion Convention committee "having this matter in charge," that is, "universal mobilization."

Colonel Markey thereupon testified that the Legion approved the drafting of "everything" and that the purpose of the agitation for "universal mobilization" is "that when you have drafted the men in every walk of life" you will also "draft cattle."

Mr. Garrett [21]—The question I wanted to ask is in regard to section A, "the draft of the material resources, industrial organization, and services over which Government control is

[21] Representative Daniel E. Garrett of Texas.

necessary to the successful termination of such emergency." Do you mean by that, now, that the purpose of this legislation is that when you have drafted the men in every walk of life that you also propose to draft cattle, for instance, and prevent profit there?

Mr. Markey—Yes, sir; absolutely.

Mr. Garrett—And that everything will be drafted when we have war, and the war will have to be fought out on a different principle than that large profits may be made and then afterwards an attempt made to get those profits back in the way of taxes?

Mr. Markey—Yes. . .[22]

Mr. E. E. Spafford, former Commander of the American Legion, in a statement made in 1927, also gave the country the impression that the Legion was agitating for the drafting of wealth and property as the Government drafts life. Former Commander Spafford stated:

Let labor and capital be conscripted at a sacrifice as well as men. Let there be no more of one man serving for $30 a month risking his life in battle, and another risking his clothing at $30 a day. Let capital serve at a similar sacrifice.

It is fair to assume, therefore, that the words of the resolution "equalizing the burdens . . . of war" meant, in the light of the Legion's own declaration, that the proponents of this resolution intended Congress to place profit on the same plane as life insofar as it is possible to reconcile the two.

22 Hearings before the Committee on Military Affairs, United States House of Representatives ("Universal Mobilization for War Purposes"), on H. J. Res. 128, H. R. 194, H. R. 4841 and H. R. 8111, 68th Cong., 1st Ses., page 20.

As in the fairy tale, the king was naked. Unlike it, he said so first. Mr. Ralph T. O'Neil, the then Commander of the American Legion and its representative before the War Policies Commission, enunciated a startling change of policy, one as close to the conscription of wealth in war-time as the notorious cost-plus War Department contract which practically gave the manufacturer and contractor an arbitrary profit based on their uncontrolled and unregulated costs.

The Commander went one per cent further than the War Department. He recommended a guaranteed return up to 7 per cent to industry in war-time. This 7 per cent, he declared, would be "a fair return." He restated the resolution adopted by the American Legion in 1922. "That policy," he said to the War Policies Commission, "is as follows:"

> That there should be a universal draft of not only the man power, but of the material resources of our country; first, so that it would lessen materially the future possibility of war; and further, that if such a national emergency did present itself to the Nation, we would be prepared with an orderly, comprehensive plan to mobilize the entire resources of the whole country without respect to any conditions that would limit the full use of the full power of our Nation.[23]

The Commander added that this Legion resolution "is a simple statement of the American Legion's principle and the organization has always been back of that particular

[23] War Policies Commission Hearings, page 8.

principle." In making a definite recommendation to the Commission Mr. O'Neil said:

> Now, the question is, what can this Commission do—how can you accomplish anything? Legislation should be recommended which should provide for the immediate mobilization of the resources of our Nation. That would mean the mobilization of men, money, materials, and food; the fixing of all prices, which means the fixing of the prices of labor also, and the regulation and distribution of production. The military authorities should put into effect the draft of the entire population, from which the required number of men should be drawn, and place the necessary orders for equipment and material. Prices of materials, commodities, and, in fact, all things, should be declared fixed as of a definite date, and it should be illegal either to buy or sell at a different price.
>
> The machinery to make this effective could immediately be set up as was done during the World War through State councils of defense. A price-fixing committee should immediately be set up to function wherever and whenever necessary. We do not want to draft capital and we do not want to draft labor, but we want absolute control over both by the Government. We want this control right at the beginning of any war that we might have; we do not want the control over labor, for instance, to take place after the shipyards have raised the pay of their men from $1.50 a day to $14 a day or whatever it was. We want that control exercised at the start, so that the men who have to go into the armed service shall not pay a greater percentage of their income for the actual necessities of life than those who will remain behind and serve our Nation in the ways of industry.[24]

There seems to be a conflict of opinion between the

[24] *Ibid.*, page 11.

words of the 1922 Legion resolution and Commander O'Neil's interpretation of them.

In answer to a question relative to the meaning of "universal draft," Mr. O'Neil let the cat out of the bag.

> I do not think you need any constitutional action in any event. Of course, I do not think "universal draft" is a very good name for any legislation that might be enacted. We used it because it has been a popular name.[25]

He further admonished the Commission that "there must be no exemption under the basic law." His words dropped into the bottomless pit of political rhetoric——

> The entire man power of the country without stint or limitation must be subjected to the call of the country for military or industrial service, without distinction as to wage paid for similar classes of effort. There must be no exemption under the basic law. All of the material resources of the Nation must similarly be subject to the call of the Nation without stint.

A Seven Per Cent War

"Without stint," as far as capital and wealth are concerned, under this "basic law" evidently means a guarantee of 7 per cent.

In reviewing Mr. O'Neil's testimony, especially on the guarantee to industry of a 7 per cent return, one cannot help but conclude that either the Legionnaires were jesting or that he, a lawyer who represents several railroads, did not speak as the true representative of the Legion rank and file.

[25] *Ibid.*, page 14.

Mr. Collins—And what you regard as fair compensation, as I have understood your testimony, would be the same level of profits that obtain in peace time?

Mr. O'Neil—Yes; generally speaking.

Mr. Collins—And if one corporation should be making nothing today and another one should be making 100 per cent, you would pay them the same level of profits they are receiving in peace time?

Mr. O'Neil—No; I said, generally speaking, a fair compensation.

Mr. Collins—Well, what I want to find out is what you mean by "same level of profits"?

Mr. O'Neil—All right; let me illustrate: What is the railroad entitled to receive?

Mr. Collins—That is what I want you to tell me.

Mr. O'Neil—Well, it is entitled to receive a fair return on its investment. That is what the law is now, irrespective of any universal draft act.

Mr. Collins—Well, some receive one amount and some receive another.

Mr. O'Neil—Oh, no.

Mr. Collins—Oh, yes.

Mr. O'Neil—Not theoretically.

Mr. Collins—Do you mean theoretically? I mean actually.

Mr. O'Neil—They are permitted to receive a maximum amount and that only—any railroad. We are getting a little bit off of the subject, because that is a public utility, but that is what they are entitled to receive on their investment—a fair return. No railroad is entitled to receive more than that. Now, I think that should apply in case of war to all industries—some similar principle.

Mr. Collins—Well, would you fix 6 per cent, 8 per cent, or 10 per cent?

Mr. O'Neil—Well, taking the railroad for illustration again, a good many courts have said 6 per cent is a fair return upon the investment.

Mr. Collins—Some public utility commissions have said a higher amount than that.

Mr. O'Neil—Well, they have never said over 8 per cent.

Mr. Collins—Well, what would you say?

Mr. O'Neil—I would say probably 7 per cent was fair.[26]

The head of the organization which, after ten years' agitation, was instrumental in securing the creation of a joint Congressional commission for the purpose of considering amending the Constitution so that private property could be taken by Congress for public use during war, informed his own child that he was uncertain of his constitutional opinion inasmuch as he did not have "a chance to give it the proper thought"! After a decade of agitation for drafting the "dollar," he, as the Legion's representative, desired only to take "the exploitation profits out of war," to eliminate "profiteering; that is, unreasonable and excessive profits."

Mr. Collins—In other words, your idea is that instead of taking the profits out of war, you ought to yield to industry in time of war a certain return on their investment. That is your idea, boiled down, as I see it?

Mr. O'Neil—Yes. If we do not change this constitutional provision, you have to do that.

Mr. Collins—And you are not proposing an amendment to the Constitution?

Mr. O'Neil—No; I want to limit that again by saying I am not really so certain of my opinion on the constitutional law, because I have not had a chance to give it the proper thought;

[26] *Ibid.*, page 21.

but, if the law is as I think it is, I certainly would not propose a constitutional amendment.

Mr. Collins—And in event of war, you think they ought to be paid up to 7 per cent?

Mr. O'Neil—That is a fair return; yes. If they do not get any more than that, it will help considerably. That is a maximum, you understand?

Senator Vandenberg—You are talking about taking the exploitation profits out of war?

Mr. O'Neil—That is what I am trying to do.

Mr. McSwain—In other words, eliminating what is ordinarily called profiteering; that is, unreasonable and excessive profits?

Mr. O'Neil—Yes.[27]

Other veterans' representatives made similar contributions. Mr. Thomas Kirby, National Chairman of the Disabled American Veterans, advised the Commission to draft labor as you do the soldier but pay capital "a reasonable return upon their investment." Mr. Paul V. McNutt,[28] former Commander of the American Legion

[27] *Ibid.*, page 28.

[28] In the Senate investigation of the activities of the notorious William B. Shearer at the Geneva Naval Conference in 1927, as a paid representative of shipbuilding concerns, Mr. Shearer testified:

> The former national commander of the American Legion—Commander Spafford, formerly of the United States Navy—wrote a letter to John Thomas Taylor, who is the attorney representing the Legion here, saying, "You had better get Bill Shearer down there to post the new commander—McNutt—who is to make a speech at the Mayflower Hotel before the Sojourners." With that letter, I came down to Washington, and I entered Commander McNutt's apartment and was with him until 3 in the morning, educating him, we will say, or posting him, or whatever you wish. . . . Therefore, I was pronounced by the national commander of the American Legion as the best-posted man

and present Dean of the Law School of the Indiana University, defined "equalizing the burdens of war" as merely preventing "undue profit."

> Mr. Collins—Well, what do you mean by equalizing the burdens of war, then?
> Mr. McNutt—Keeping them on the same level, in order that the happening of a war will not bring to any person any undue profit.
> Mr. Collins—Well, you merely mean, then, by the equalizing of the burdens of war, paying people the same salaries and wages and the same prices for articles that were in vogue prior to the existence of war?
> Mr. McNutt—Certainly.[29]

"Labor" Studies "the Economics of the Situation"

Curiously enough, on the question of the percentage rate to be paid capital in war-time, Mr. William Green, president of the American Federation of Labor, was in striking agreement with the American Legion representatives who

in the United States on national defense. I have the letter. . . . The next night Commander McNutt made his famous speech. I had given him all the data that I thought was necessary to carry on the policy of the American Legion, which had just adopted a resolution to build these cruisers. When I returned to New York, I called up Mr. Willicomb, Mr. Hearst's private secretary, and said I had received a letter from Commander McNutt expressing himself not only for the Navy but opposed to the World Court, and if Mr. Hearst thought it was right, I believed that the patriotic organizations would take the same stand as the American Legion. (Hearings before a Subcommittee of the Committee on Naval Affairs, United States Senate ["Alleged Activities at the Geneva Conference"], 71st Cong., 1st Ses., pursuant to S. Res. 114, page 539.)

[29] War Policies Commission Hearings, page 215.

appeared before the War Policies Commission. It is difficult to regard his testimony as disputing any of the fundamental tenets of the economic status quo as related to prospective "war policies."

Mr. Green also seemed to agree with Mr. Daniel Willard, president of the Baltimore and Ohio Railroad, who, with his usual refreshing lucidity,[30] informed the Commission: ". . . I do not think it is right to take a man's property and use it for any purpose for the good of all of us and not let him make a reasonable profit. That, I think, he is entitled to in war, peace, or any other time."[31]

Mr. Green, after studying "the economics of the situation," gave the Commission the benefit of his research.

> Mr. Green—I think we all agree, everyone who has studied the economics of the situation, that industry and capital are entitled to a fair return upon their investment under any circumstances—in times of war or times of peace.[32]

The President of the American Federation of Labor would "take the profit out of war," that is, eliminate "profiteering," through the medium of "heavy war-profits taxes." He also testified that he would establish "flexible" price-control organizations which "must of necessity follow a policy sufficiently flexible to meet the requirements and the needs of these shifting, changing, economic conditions."

[30] Mr. Willard, speaking at the fiftieth anniversary of the founding of the Wharton School of Commerce and Finance of the University of Pennsylvania, on March 27, 1931, stated that if unemployed he would steal rather than starve.

[31] War Policies Commission Hearings, pages 185–86.

[32] *Ibid.*, page 277.

> I think, of course, it is most reprehensible that men should profit as a result of war. The theory of preventing profiteering is correct. It ought to be prevented; but I think any thinking man will realize how difficult it is to do that in a practical and successful way. My own opinion is that the practical way to regulate that feature of it, to take the profit out of war, would be for the Government to recapture the profits through the imposition of heavy war-profits taxes. I doubt that there is any other way. Of course, there must be some price control, through the establishment of price-control organizations; but, at the same time, those price-control organizations must of necessity follow a policy sufficiently flexible to meet the requirements and the needs of these shifting, changing, economic conditions.[33]

It is difficult to reconcile Mr. Green's approval of war-profits taxes with the general knowledge of their lamentable failure in the World War and with the well-known revolting story of padded payrolls, thinly disguised bribery and out-and-out lying.[34]

[33] *Ibid.*, pages 274–75.

[34] Representative McSwain referred to a glaring case of war profiteering during his cross-examination of Mr. Newton D. Baker, former Secretary of War:

> Mr. McSwain—Now, did you ever hear during the war of the name of the American Metal Co., of New York?
>
> Mr. Baker—No, sir; not that I recall.
>
> Mr. McSwain—In that same report Mr. Colver [Chairman of the Federal Trade Commission during the War and also a member of the price-fixing committee of the War Industries Board] reported that everybody in that corporation—from the chairman of the board of trustees on down—had been paid bonuses for the purpose of hiding the profits. The president of the company received a bonus over and above his salary of $364,000 in one year, and it went all the way down to the foremen of the shops. The chief engineer got $23,500 bonus, the manager of gas operation got $7,000 bonus, and here is a list of about

It is to be presumed that Mr. Edward F. McGrady, the present legislative representative of the American Federation of Labor and the official who represented the Federation before the "Universal Mobilization for War Purposes" Commission in 1924, had "studied the economics of the situation." Nevertheless, his conclusions to this study contradict those of Mr. Green, the American Federation of Labor representative, as now presented seven years later before the War Policies Commission.[35] Mr. McGrady proposed that in case of war all should "get in the same boat."

Briefly, our position is this: That we are opposed to any profits being made in war time by war contractors. We also believe that everything should be done to try to prevent any wars in the future; and we are willing to go on a $30-a-month

20 different officers and clerks of the corporation that got a total of nearly $2,000,000 bonus for the purpose of hiding as overhead expenses a part of these very war profits. Now, it seems to me, if our boys had known that such as that was going on, it would have affected very seriously their morale. That is the reason why the boys who did the fighting, when they got back home and found out what had happened, raised up in arms, through the American Legion and through other patriotic organizations, and demanded, in event of another war, every human ingenuity and every reasonable effort should be resorted to in advance to prevent a recurrence of that very thing. Now, can you conceive of anything that would be more calculated to stimulate a righteous morale among the people than a sense of justice among the people as to their being justly treated under war conditions? (War Policies Commission Hearings, page 132.)

For specific amounts paid by the American Metal Co. (Ltd.), of New York, see document No. 248, 65th Cong., 2nd Ses., "A letter from the chairman of the Federal Trade Commission in response to a Senate Resolution of June 10, 1918, transmitting a report containing all facts, figures, data, or information now in possession of the Federal Trade Commission relative to profiteering," pages 7–8.

35 "Today the A. F. of L. is utterly spiritless. Its leaders are pompous,

basis, and we are ready and willing to eat Army rations, when you can make the brokers and bankers and the business men and the war contractors and Members of Congress and Members of the Supreme Court do the same thing. Let us all get in the same boat.[86]

Mr. McGrady, in spite of or because of his study of "the economics of the situation," testified that he would also take the profit "out of war materials during peace-times, absolutely. Why not?"

Mr. Hull—What do you think about the possibility of stopping profiteering during war if we find it impossible to stop profiteering in peace times in munitions of war?

Mr. McGrady—Well, Congressman, I believe that you have brought out a very vital subject. I believe the profits should be taken out of war materials during peace times, absolutely. Why not?

Mr. Hull—Well, that is my thought, and I wanted to know yours.

Mr. McGrady—That is my thought, too. If we need munitions of war, if we need guns, etc., in peace time, why can not the Government do that? Why can not they make the guns? Why can not they make the powder? Why can not

high-toned Babbitts, some of them with stock-exchange tickers in their offices. Its conventions compare with those of the Elks, the Rotarians, and the National Association of Soap Manufacturers. They invite Army generals to address them. William Green, Gompers's worthy successor, goes to West Point to review the cadet corps and receive honors such as are ordinarily rendered only to visiting royalty, while in Massachusetts they let Sacco and Vanzetti go to the chair and in California Tom Mooney, a trade unionist, stays in prison for fourteen years although innocent of the crime for which he was convicted."—From *Dynamite,* by Louis Adamic, Viking Press, pages 251–52.

[86] Hearings on "Universal Mobilization for War Purposes," *op. cit.,* page 79.

they do other things, in order that all profits might be taken out?

Mr. Frothingham—Utilize the arsenals and the navy yards?

Mr. McGrady—Absolutely, and they can do it, in my estimation, cheaper than it is being done by private contract.

Mr. Frothingham—Well, some ships have been built in the navy yards, have they not?

Mr. McGrady—Yes.

Mr. Frothingham—If they had used them in the last few years more than they ever had done before, I do not know.

Mr. McGrady—Well, we have been trying to get the Government to agree to let the navy yards bid on reconditioning the ships, and I think we have had a rather unfortunate experience in that, because we have not been able to get anything. You are familiar with this, I know.

I might call your attention to what happened with the *Leviathan*. There is the Boston Navy Yard, a Government plant, ready and equipped, and they put a bid in lower than the private contractors, to get the job, but they could not get it.

Mr. Frothingham—Yes; and they ought to have had the contract.[37]

And so, it seems reasonably and tragically certain that appreciable profits will not be unduly disturbed in case we should be so unfortunate as to be drawn into another war, if the convictions of certain representatives of labor, capital and property, veterans' organizations and the War Department should still be a decisively dominant part of our political and economic organism.

Nevertheless, it is unmistakable that the popular demand which resulted in the resolution under which this Com-

[37] *Ibid.*, pages 80–81.

mission sat was a demand to draft capital as the Government drafts men. Any attempt to say that this huge sentiment was merely directed toward the elimination of "war profits," that is, those profits above the so-called normal rate, is crass misrepresentation. The fact that there may be difficulties in the execution of such a desire does not excuse the falsifying of the precise nature of that desire.[38]

[38] The National Grange, one of the leading farmers' organizations, seems to have had no difficulty in understanding the resolution. At its sixty-fifth annual session at Madison, Wisconsin, in November 1931, it adopted the following resolution:

> *Conscription of Wealth*—Resolved, that we favor the enactment of a law making it mandatory in case of war, to draft resources of individuals and corporations as well as men.

CHAPTER THREE

THE WAR DEPARTMENT GENERAL MOBILIZATION PLAN

The post-war orgy of hysterical nationalism was chiefly responsible for the National Defense Act of 1920. Jingo speeches and editorials, "patriotic" breast-beating and the Red-baiting raids of Attorney-General A. Mitchell Palmer apparently convinced Congress that legislation should be passed which would keep the country in a perpetual state of readiness for war at a moment's notice.

The National Defense Act of 1920, as amended June 4, 1924, aside from its purely technical and military provisions, attempts to provide for the organization of production in the country's industries so that a sufficient number of troops for a major war can be supplied promptly on the outbreak of hostilities with all the materials necessary for waging war. It virtually amounts to mobilization of the basic industries of the country.

Under this Act the Assistant Secretary of War was ordered to card-index the production facilities of the United States. Section 5a charges him, under the direction of the Secretary of War, with the "supervision of the procurement of all military supplies and other business of the War Department pertaining thereto and the assurance of adequate provision for the mobilization of matériel and industrial organizations essential to war-time needs."

That part of the Mobilization Plan prepared by the War Department under this Act was read to the Commission. It dealt with the filling of prearranged contracts, with profiteering and price, plans and studies affecting raw materials and the total war organization of national industry.

Cross-examination was centered chiefly on two points, the danger of peace-time militarization of industry, and the 6 per cent war-time profit to industry by the War Department.

As far as any definite proposal of the entire mobilization plan of the War Department to Congress by the Commission is concerned, it is important to remember that General MacArthur, the War Department's spokesman, agreed that his recommendation for endorsement of the plan went beyond the scope of the Commission's designated authority.

Mr. Collins—General MacArthur, you remember that the resolution creating this commission charged it with considering that private property may be taken by Congress for public use during war and with methods for equalizing the burdens and removing the profits of war. Your recommendation has gone beyond that, and contains some additional considerations.

General MacArthur—Yes.

Mr. Collins—Your conclusion would be what lawyers would call ultra vires?

General MacArthur—Yes. I am not a lawyer, but I know what ultra vires means.

Mr. Collins—In other words, beyond the scope of our authority.

General MacArthur—Yes.

Mr. Collins—And in addition to that you are asking us to give our approval to these proposals, and also to use our influence toward getting Congress to give its approval in one form or another to these proposals of yours.

General MacArthur—Hardly that.

Mr. Collins—You stated that you wanted a resolution passed by Congress putting the stamp of approval upon your recommendations, generally, if I heard you correctly.

General MacArthur—Generally, yes.[39]

Nevertheless, a study of the cross-examination of General MacArthur immediately after his lengthy presentation of the War Department Mobilization Plan gives one a deep insight into the purely military concept of a problem for whose consideration the Commission was created. More positively, it gives one a clear idea of what sort of economic program the War Department may be expected to urge or fasten upon the Government in the event of war.

"Profiteering and other injustices," General MacArthur averred, are part of "the evils the plans and preparations of the War Department are intended to prevent."

General MacArthur's conception of the elimination of profiteering, according to the Commission record, is the payment of a price which would result in a profit to industry of a sum not in excess of 6 per cent and the framing of tax laws which "should be so framed as to require the minimum of inflation, and to recapture all unusual profits."[40] This profit, the General testified, would be based "on what it is claimed is the investment."[41]

[39] War Policies Commission Hearings, page 380.

[40] The ease with which business concerns can escape tax collection is told briefly in the Federal Trade Commission reports and especially in Mr. McSwain's questioning of Mr. Baruch, already referred to.

[41] *See* above, page 20f.

Mr. Collins—Anyway, from the standpoint of profit, if we had another war, you would try to make the profit 6 per cent instead of 50 or 60 per cent?

General MacArthur—We recommend 6 per cent, but that is open to discussion.[42]

It is impossible to escape the conclusion that a profit of 6 per cent based "on what it is claimed is the investment," agreed upon by the representatives of industry and the War Department, is little improvement upon the vicious and terribly expensive cost-plus system for both the marginal and low cost producer. It is also inescapable that reduction of the recommended 6 per cent which would retain the principle of the program, would merely provide another opportunity for corporation accountants to hide profits in more ingenious ways than during the World War.

The vague suggestion for tax legislation to "recapture all unusual profits," in the face of the complete failure of the government to "recapture" them in the last war, is evidence of either an inexcusable ignorance of the public facts or a tacit willingness to allow the repetition of such unconscionable thievery at the general expense.

Commissioning 14,000 "Patriotic Industrialists"

It is a matter of record that the War Department, presumably under Section 5a of the National Defense Act, has commissioned at least 14,000 key industrialists in the reserve forces of the United States Army.

[42] War Policies Commission Hearings, pages 383–84.

Secretary Hurley—In regard to the industrial service of the Army, to which Congressman Collins has alluded, you are aware, of course, that a plan for industrial mobilization is necessary under the national defense act?

Mr. Willard—Yes.

Secretary Hurley—And that approximately 14,000 industrialists throughout the Nation have taken reserve officers' commissions, and that some of these, in conjunction with officers of the Army charged with that responsibility, have developed an industrial mobilization plan in the War Department? [43]

* * * * *

General MacArthur—I think it pertinent also to say here that the voluntary assistance we constantly receive from other departments, from associations, and from patriotic industrialists, is of the utmost value and fully appreciated by the Government. We are studying ways and means through which this assistance may be more efficiently organized—and so facilitate crystallization of information and opinion, and promote mutual understanding of these important subjects.[44]

Mention of the country's industrialists is worth a brief digression on the career of Charles M. Schwab, chairman of the Board of Directors of the Bethlehem Steel Corporation, a founder of the Navy League and one of the nation's most powerful industrial magnates. Mr. Schwab's connection with the Government's war plans and activities began as early as 1894. The House of Representatives Report, No. 1468, Fifty-Third Congress, second session, entitled "Violation of Armor Plate Contracts," gives an account of this connection. This report followed an investigation in 1894

[43] *Ibid.*, page 188.
[44] *Ibid.*, page 376.

by the House Committee on Naval Affairs into charges of fraud against the Carnegie Steel Company, then Carnegie, Phipps & Co. Mr. Schwab, then General Superintendent of the Carnegie Steel Company, admitted to the Committee that he gave orders that "blow holes" in armor plate should not mean rejection of the plate. He testified that it was "likely" that his company "did really conceal the fact of blowholes in the plate." (Page 647.)

Mr. William E. Corey, the president of the Midvale Steel and Ordnance Company[45] and a director of the International Nickel Company, was in charge of the armor plant in which the frauds were committed. On the stand Mr. Corey testified: (Page 559.)

Q. Did anybody above you—did any superior officer—know that you were doing this thing?—A. Yes, sir.

Q. Who was it?—A. Mr. Schwab knew about it in a general way.

Q. Did anybody else?—A. No, sir.

The official House Report condemned this unconscionable act in no uncertain terms:

The servants of the Carnegie Steel Co. (whether with or without the knowledge of the company), to increase their gains,

[45] Page 32 of the February 1904 issue of the *Navy League Journal*, the "official organ of the Navy League," lists the Midvale Steel Company and Robert M. Thompson, the then chairman of the Board of Directors of the International Nickel Company, among the nineteen founders of the Navy League. The other founders there listed are: Herbert L. Satterlee, J. W. Miller, J. Pierpont Morgan, Benjamin F. Tracy, Seth Low, Clement A. Griscom, Thomas Lowry, Timothy L. Woodruff, Anson Phelps Stokes, George Westinghouse, R. S. Sloan, John J. Astor, John J. McCook, Harry Payne Whitney, George B. Satterlee, and S. S. Palmer.

deliberately continued for many months to commit acts whose natural and probable consequence would be the sacrifice of the lives of our seamen in time of war, and with them, perhaps, the dearest interests of the Nation. . .

No fine or mere money compensation is an adequate atonement for such wrongs. The commission of such frauds is a moral crime of the gravest character . . .

President Cleveland assessed damages of $140,000 against the Carnegie Steel Company in spite of the vigorous protests made to him by Philander C. Knox, General Counsel for the Carnegie Steel Company and later Attorney-General and Secretary of State of the United States. These damages were paid *immediately.*

In 1930, before a subcommittee of the Committee on Naval Affairs of the United States Senate, Mr. Schwab testified that he was unaware of the employment of the notorious William B. Shearer by his company until "this question came out." Mr. Schwab informed the Committee that his interest in the Geneva Arms Conference, during the sessions of which Mr. Shearer labored for several arms and shipbuilding companies including the Bethlehem Steel Corporation, could be attributed to his love of peace. "I was interested in a way that I wanted to see peace come to the world, and especially to this own great country of ours; no entanglements of war. Not only was I interested as a patriotic American citizen, but I may say that I was selfishly interested from a prosperity point of view of this great country, particularly as an industrial country under peaceful conditions."

The suit of Mr. Shearer—he boasted that he had wrecked the Geneva Arms Conference—against several shipbuilding and armament concerns is still pending in the New York state courts.[46]

Mr. Schwab during the World War, from April to December of 1918, was the Director General of the United States Shipping Board Emergency Fleet Corporation. In this capacity, as one of the numerous dollar-a-year patriots, he superintended the making of huge government shipbuilding contracts.

In view of the fact that the certainty of increased profits is usually a sufficient stimulus to elicit the cooperation of the country's "patriotic industrialists" there is reason to believe that other motives actuated the adoption of a policy of commissioning such industrialists in the reserve corps of the army.

According to the General Mobilization Plan of the War Department read to the Commission

> (f) The prices promulgated as fair and reasonable should be determined by agreement between Government and the representatives of industry. . . .[47]

When it is remembered that these men become regular officers of the War Department in the event of war one realizes with fear and amazement the danger and true significance of the War Department's "agency to determine prices for general governmental buying." This—profit

[46] *See* note 28.

[47] General Mobilization Plan of the War Department, War Policies Commission Hearings, page 372.

strengthened by the sword—is the case despite the attempt of General MacArthur to establish the contrary opinion.

There seems to exist a wrong impression as to the use that the Army intends to make of its reserve officers in war. None of them will be left in industry. Reserve officers in war must necessarily sever their business connections and will have exactly the same status, for the time being, as do the Regular Army officers. No one in the War Department will exercise any operating control of any character over privately owned and operated industrial establishments other than that which is involved in the specific performance of contractual terms.[48]

It is not in the scheme of things that the fraud and chicanery common to business in peace-time will disappear during a period when its operation is least difficult to cloak. Furthermore, the "operating control" can be left to others as long as dictation of "contractual terms" is retained.

These industrialists, who are given to understand by General MacArthur and the War Department that this "industrial plan assures that the Government itself will not unnecessarily upset economic and industrial conditions," will have the armed forces of the United States—in all probability, conscripted and paid one dollar a day—to enforce their own decisions which will automatically repay their "patriotism" at a profit of 6 per cent! One can easily understand the War Department's provision that "prices promulgated as fair and reasonable should be determined by agreement between Government and the representatives of industry."

[48] *Ibid.*, page 367.

Thus, the War Department's mobilization plan, ostensibly opposed to profiteering, will identify itself with the forces to which it professes to be opposed for the simple reason that the 14,000 industrialists are the very people who will administer the War Department's "agency to determine prices for general governmental buying." This condition is not helped by the fact that these 14,000 industrialists now hold reserve commissions in the United States Army.

Nor is it helped by the fact that human greed, especially when privileged, offers not the slightest hope that these individuals will be content with the War Department's exceedingly generous provision for a 6 per cent profit.

The Militarization of Industry

The War Department is intent upon creating a "super-agency" under its auspices which would, in the words of Colonel Robbins, "enable the President to exercise intelligent leadership over the industrial resources of the Nation," which would "fix the price of all important commodities, including labor," and assure "the Government contractor" a "reasonable profit."

Though repeatedly denied by the Secretary of War the facts show that the War Department is pursuing a program which, if unchecked, means eventual militarization of industry. If the War Department Mobilization Plan should be completed in its present form the military arm of the Government will be put in such potential control of industry as to take over the country's plants, factories, fields, and transportation systems in the shortest possible time in case of what the War Department designates "a national emergency declared by Congress to exist, which, in the judgment of the President demands the immediate increase of the armed forces of the United States."[49]

What transpired at one of Mr. Baruch's annual War College lectures at which the Commandant of the War College opposed the right of any civilian to determine what should be done by industry, emphatically contradicts the denial of the Secretary of War that the present War Department Mobilization Plan means the militarization of industry, according to Congressman McSwain's contribution during the questioning of Mr. Baruch.

Mr. Baruch—My answer is this: that I do not believe that the military ought to run industries; but they ought to know something about the way they are run, so that, when industry has to meet their problems, there will be a mutual understanding of the problems. They will at least then know how to talk each other's language.

Mr. Collins—But you do not believe in the militarization of industry?

Mr. Baruch—I do not; nor the industrialization of the Army.

Secretary Hurley—I may ask, do you know of any one inter-

[49] The administrative committee of the Federal Council of the Churches of Christ in America, in a "Statement Regarding the Conscription of Life, Labor, and Capital," which was mailed to each member of the Commission and read publicly on May 13, 1931, in section 4 of the statement, said:

> 4. We regard the adoption by Congress in times of assured and prolonged peace of detailed and comprehensive plans for the potential, complete, and instantaneous war-time control by the United States Army of the country's industrial, commercial, and transportation systems as fraught with grave dangers to our country. (War Policies Commission Hearings, page 354.)

ested in this problem who does believe in the militarization of industry?

Mr. Baruch—I do not know of any and, if I did, I should fight them as long as the power rests in me.[50]

Mr. McSwain thereupon refreshed Mr. Baruch's memory.

Mr. McSwain—But the witness remembers, at a certain lecture he delivered at the War College, there was considerable sentiment manifested on the part of the then commandant of the War College in opposition to the sentiments just expressed by the witness, who said that the civilian power, as he has said here to-day, should always determine what should be done by industry, the priority in which commodities should be supplied and transported, and the commandant of the War College remonstrated, with great energy and vigor, that any civilian should ever be permitted to tell the military establishment when and what it should do, and you combatted that with great effect.

Mr. Baruch—Yes, sir.

Mr. McSwain—And are still combatting it.

Mr. Baruch—The only thing the military should say is what they want, because they have to fight with it; they should say what they want and when they want it and sign the contract, and inspect it and use it; but it is for the industrialists to say where they should get it and the conditions under which they should get it and, in getting it, protect the civilian population in its necessities. To my mind the line of demarcation is perfectly plain, but I can see no objection to the military man studying industry, and particularly a man who might be a shop man, any more than I can see objection to the industrialists studying the military viewpoint, in order to be able to meet on a common ground, with a common language.

[50] *Ibid.*, page 68.

Mr. McSwain—The distinguished gentleman who has been so greatly informing us by his experience, insisted at that address which I attended, as I always attend any occasion where the distinguished gentleman is to speak, if I have the opportunity, maintained there with the same energy that he does today, that the civilian authority should always remain in control of industry, and that labor should never be conscripted; but I simply call the attention of the gentleman and those present to the fact that there was a contrary view expressed at that time among certain personnel present, and that we must be constantly on the alert for fear that view should trespass beyond its proper bounds.

Mr. Baruch—Quite right, sir; yes, sir.[51]

Mr. Baruch, in his lengthy pamphlet on "Taking the Profit Out of War," informed the Commission that "it is absolutely impracticable for the War Department to control industrial mobilization" and that "we must neither militarize industry nor industrialize the army."

In stating his objections to such War Department control, he said:

It is impracticable to maintain in peace any such powerful agency as is necessary in war to administer the gigantic effort of national economic mobilization. We should prepare a complete plan for such an organization but even that must be in the broadest of terms. It is impossible to foresee the precise circumstance and requirements of any future war. Perhaps a skeleton organization might be provided for—merely to insure the development of a personnel. The Congress has attempted to do this by making the Assistant Secretary of War responsible for making plans for industrial mobilization. Devoted work

[51] *Ibid.*, page 69.

has been done in the War Department but there is some danger in this method. It is absolutely impracticable for the War Department to control industrial mobilization because

(a) It is an economic problem requiring the ablest leadership in industry and utterly unsuited to military administration;

(b) The central control agency must act as arbiter of conflicting demands—the greatest of which is that of the civilian population. No single competitor such as the War Department should be intrusted with such arbitration;

(c) The job of the War Department is our armed forces. That is a big job. To pile on top of it the task of economic mobilization would insure the failure of both.

There is an inevitable tendency in the War Department to forget these principles even in planning. Their function is to say what they want and when and where they want it. The job of industrial control is to see that they get it strictly on their specification. We must neither militarize industry nor industrialize the Army. While I do not advocate change in the present law, the facts just stated should forever be borne in mind.[52]

Several other important military, financial and industrial figures agreed with Mr. Baruch on the general principle that "it is impossible to foresee the precise circumstance and requirements of any future war" and that therefore the passage of specific legislation or the adoption of detailed war plans might not only waste time and money but also impede the drawing up of necessary plans when the occasion should arise.

Mr. Eugene Meyer, Jr., Governor of the Federal Reserve

[52] *Ibid.*, page 38.

Board, in discussing the financial aspect of that opinion, declared:

The details of financing and financial control can not be planned in advance, for the reason that it will depend upon the kind and scope of the war and economic, social, and political conditions of the nation involved, and at the time, furthermore, financial problems do not function like automatic machines under the hand of any operator, but, even more than any other phase of the war problem, their successful solution is dependent upon the men available to operate the financial agencies. Therefore, to a considerable measure, financial agencies and controls must be adjusted to the men who are available to operate them.[53]

* * * * *

Secretary Hurley—Mr. Meyer, during your study of this problem have you arrived at a conclusion as to what law or laws should be enacted now, under which to guide the fiscal policies of the Nation in another emergency, should one occur?

Mr. Meyer—I have not studied the matter of legislation from the point of view of anticipating war, Mr. Secretary. The Congress certainly will be in session if there is any war, and I have the feeling that any legislation which might be prepared in a general way could be pointed up in its detail more effectively at the time than it could be in advance of a war, the scope and circumstances of which can not be anticipated. Of course, some fundamental legislation might be thought out; but I believe that, so far as the major requirements are concerned, legislation can be passed promptly enough when the time comes. . . .

Secretary Hurley—You are rather of the opinion, I take it, the policy should not be enacted now, but should be left to the determination of those who have to conduct the war?

[53] *Ibid.*, pages 232–33.

Mr. Meyer—It seems to me that would be the better plan. I feel, gentlemen, there is no immediate prospect of war. I do not see any wars coming for a long time, because, apart from anything else, one great lesson has been learned from the last war, which perhaps never was learned so thoroughly before, and that is that war is a profitless operation to all peoples—winners as well as losers. That has been made so clear that I think it is the greatest deterrent of war; but I would not want to say, on the other hand, that there never will be any war. But every 5 or 10 years brings great changes, economically, financially, and otherwise. Certainly, if there were to be a war in this period, with the developments which have taken place ever since the last war, the changed conditions would make it a very different operation. So that in anticipating a war which may not develop, and which I certainly hope will not develop for a considerable time at least, it would be very difficult, I think, to visualize the conditions under which such a war would have to be carried on. It would be quite impossible, it seems to me, to make very effective plans now in any detail.[54]

Mr. Augustus H. Griswold, Vice-President of the International Telegraph and Telephone Company, in discussing the problem from the angle of communications, told the Commission that "the laying down of detailed specific plans, by legislative act or otherwise, would appear to be not only a waste of both time and money but might actually prevent the prompt establishment of correct plans for a particular emergency when and as it arose." [55]

[54] *Ibid.*, pages 238-39.

[55] This point brings up the proposal made to the Commission by both Admiral Samuel McGowan and Dr. Thomas Hall Shastid for a constitutional amendment which would necessitate the holding of a national referendum, except in the event of attack or invasion, before declaring

Mr. Newton D. Baker, voicing a military-economic point of view, stated that:

> As a war progresses under modern conditions the inventive faculty of the various nations is stimulated, its industrial capacity is developed, and these new agencies and new theories of combat necessarily change the whole character of it. I think this is also true about the economic situation. At the outset the economic demands of a war, no matter how imaginatively they are tried to be foreseen, are varied and changed to correspond with the other changes that go on in the making of the war itself. Having had that experience, my own very strong feeling is that there is only a limited amount of preparatory economic legislation or planning that can be done and that it would be a mistake to have inelastic provisions of that sort attempted, just as it would be a mistake to have inelastic provisions made for arms.[56]

Scratching the Back of Labor

The War Department Mobilization Plan provides for the drafting of all men between the ages of 18 and 45. As far as labor is concerned, however, the War Department, under the heading "Labor in War," judiciously states that "effective use of labor in industry, in war-time as in peace-time, can be had only through labor's voluntary cooperation." This section goes on to say:

war. Although this proposal has some distinct advantages, it is generally conceded to be impracticable unless adopted by all nations. In a letter written by Charles A. Beard to Representative Collins the historian holds that "if history is any guide, declarations of war are mere formalities. To put a provision for a referendum in our Constitution would be to cripple our power for negotiation and action and would not free us from aggression if another country were bent on attacking us."

[56] War Policies Commission Hearings, page 122.

> Any system of forced labor, either by conscription or otherwise, could result only in failure. It would not be supported by public opinion and, even though tolerated by a people at war, the resentment of the workers on whom it was imposed would be a direct source of inefficient operation.
>
> It is anticipated that, as the determination of peace or war rests with the elected representatives of the people, the full cooperation of labor, equally with that of other elements of the population, will be accorded to the war and to the government.
>
> Nevertheless, there will remain the need of governmental organizations to protect labor from oppression under color of the emergency and to guide labor into useful channels and to retain it therein so far as possible. This sometimes is referred to as the control of labor, but it is based entirely on securing voluntary cooperation.[57]

To understand the War Department's attitude on labor it is essential to know that the previous War Department Mobilization Plan entitled "Plan for Industrial Mobilization 1930," which was sent to members of the Commission just before the opening of the hearings, was not so solicitous of "the need of governmental organizations to protect labor from oppression under color of the emergency and to guide labor into useful channels." Rather with brusque honesty it listed the labor problems in a manner far removed from "protection."

> c. *Labor:*
>
> The problems are the settlement of labor disputes; the control of the price of labor; control of labor migrations; coordination of employment agencies; industrial exemptions. Labor

[57] *Ibid.*, page 374.

is to be represented by its natural leaders in the organization of the Director of War Industry in its War Service Committees. Many of the questions involved, however, are of such importance that an Administrator of Man Power reporting directly to the President is also indicated as being necessary. (Page 31.)

This section, specifically "the control of the price of labor" and "control of labor migrations," was attacked and described as a conscription of labor during the cross examination of Mr. Baruch.

Mr. Collins—Mr. Baruch, in answer to a question of the Secretary of War, you gave approval to the plans for industrial mobilization which I have in front of me. Have you read the industrial mobilization plan of the War Department?

Mr. Baruch—I have had that, but I have not digested it all. The plan I have before me is a diagram which General Moseley has given me showing the set-up carrying out ideas I have suggested to them.

Mr. Collins—You do not want this commission to infer you have given your approval to this plan as it has been submitted?

Mr. Baruch—I have not gone into that, so I cannot pass any judgment on that.

Mr. Collins—I did not want you to commit yourself on something I am satisfied you do not approve of.

Mr. Baruch—But I do commit myself on the general plan General Moseley has shown me, based on some suggestions I have made to him, showing the set-up of how the thing would function and, if you give us these statutory powers, I know that will function. I might change it in some respects, but I think the general idea is copying and going along the lines of our experience. I have been given that plan; the Secretary of War was good enough to give it to me, but I was so hurried in the preparation of this memorandum that I have not had an opportunity to read it. But he was good enough to give it to me.

Secretary Hurley—I wish you would look at it at your convenience, Mr. Baruch, because I think it agrees almost completely with the testimony you have given here to-day.

Mr. Collins—The reason, for instance, I asked that question, is that we turn over here to Chart No. 9 and it says:

> Functional control of labor in war. Mission: To insure that, primarily, war industries and, secondarily, industries catering to essential civilian requirements are able to secure and maintain adequate forces of labor, skilled and unskilled, to accomplish their missions.

Now, in the first place, we have functional control of labor in war in this plan. Whatever that is may be a debatable question. Second, we have missions, to insure an adequate supply of labor, and so forth. But the only commonly well-known way of insuring an adequate supply of labor is by drafting them. Later on, over here, there is furnished us a proposed bill which undertakes to draft all men. Those between certain ages would be in the Army, but it is a general draft law. From the testimony you have given, I have been led to believe that you are against the drafting of labor.

Mr. Baruch—The conscription of labor. All labor—and by "labor," I do not contemplate, I do not visualize, the narrow form of every man who labors with his hands; but in the drafting of the whole civilian population, that covers everybody—not alone the people who work with their hands, but the people who work otherwise.

Mr. Collins—I understand. I am using "draft" in the sense of conscription. I have taken your testimony to mean you are opposed to the conscription of labor.

Mr. Baruch—I do, sir; but in the draft act and "work or fight" act——

Mr. Collins—It looks to me, from the reading of this mobilization plan, that the War Department's mobilization plan has in mind the conscription of labor.

Mr. Baruch—If it does, I am opposed to it.[58]

Evidently the charge that this section implied a conscription of labor had some merit in it since it was changed, in what is at this writing the War Department General Mobilization Plan, to read:

c. *Labor.*—The assurance to industry of an adequate labor supply, both in numbers and by occupational qualifications, will require the organization of a Labor Administration with an Administrator of Labor appointed by and directly responsible to the President at its head. In addition labor will be represented in the organization of the Director of War Industry by the appointment of its natural leaders to positions on the war-service committees. Among the more important problems to be considered are the minimizing of excessive migrations of labor by an equitable distribution of war orders, the prevention of unethical competition for labor by war industries, compilation for the information of the President of lists of industrial deferments required for efficient operation of war industries, the avoidance and settlement of industrial disputes, and the coordination of employment services.[59]

Conscripting All Men Between 18 and 45

Under questioning, General MacArthur virtually admitted the contemplation by the War Department of a conscription of all men under 45 years of age, the necessary

[58] *Ibid.,* pages 70–71.
[59] *Ibid.,* page 413.

labor contingent of which would be "allocated" to its special duties by a local board.

Mr. Collins—Do you propose to draft certain men for fighting and let in voluntarily those you want to work, or do you intend to draft the workers also?

General MacArthur—The selective service act itself, of course, inducts, as we said, all necessary men between the ages of 18 and 45.

Mr. Collins—And you want them all drafted, whether they are to work or fight?

General MacArthur—There are no exemptions at all, but they are allocated.

Mr. Collins—And you could allocate the chairman of the commission to the trenches and put me in some munitions factory, provided we were both under 45 years of age.

General MacArthur—It is to prevent such imperfections of allocations that we have devised this scheme.

Mr. Collins—So your proposal would be to draft them all and then to allocate them to the activity that you think would be best suited to the individual.

General MacArthur—Not that we think but that the local board thinks.

Mr. Collins—I understand.

General MacArthur—Correct.

Mr. Collins—Then what about the pay of those that work, who do these civilian jobs? Would you pay them the same amount that you pay a flyer or a little bit more or less?

General MacArthur—I think the plan shows clearly that as far as those men who continue in industry are concerned, the Government does not attempt to undertake coordination as between the employer and the employee. The Government does undertake to arrive at a fixed and equitable value of the product that is turned out by the industrialist, with a fair margin of profit thereon, but the incidental features thereof are matters for coordination as between the employer and the employee.

Mr. Collins—You want to take back your original statement about drafting them?

General MacArthur—No, indeed. You have not understood the paper that I have read. The law provides that all men between the ages of 18 and 45 are available. We have them registered.

Mr. Collins—You called them members of an unofficial militia.

General MacArthur—That is what the law provides.

Mr. Collins—That is what you called them.

General MacArthur—All right; that is what I call them.

Mr. Collins—They are to be drafted?

General MacArthur—Yes; those are drafted that are necessary to form military units.

Mr. Collins—And then they are to be allocated to the particular agency to which they are best suited.

General MacArthur—They are not all drafted. They are all registered.

Secretary Hurley—They are all subject to draft.

General MacArthur—Yes. The men that we induct into the combat force will be drafted. The rest of the men will remain in industry and will not be under the control of the military establishment.

Mr. Collins—Then you won't draft any men except those you want to use for military service.

General MacArthur—They would all be registered and we would take only those best fitted for the front.

Mr. Collins—And as to those that you leave behind to work, you fix the price or agree upon the price for the commodities that they produce, and you make your agreements with the heads of the organizations or with the owner or the manager of those organizations, and their labor would receive the labor price fixed in the agreements or taken into consideration when the agreements were made.

General MacArthur—That is absolutely correct.

Mr. Collins—And then those men, if the wage were unfair, would have to abide thereby until Congress or some properly empowered agency gave them a fair wage? That would be your method of handling the labor situation, would it?

General MacArthur—I specifically said that Congress would not handle the prices.

Mr. Collins—In your statement you speak of voluntary agreements with labor.

General MacArthur—Exactly.

Mr. Collins—And that, as I understand it, would preclude the right to strike.

General MacArthur—Of course you are going far afield in asking an Army man to discuss the subject of strikes and all of the ramifications that the Supreme Court of the United States has wrestled with in the last 50 years; but I can assure you that, as far as the purpose of this board is concerned, it is to leave the relationship between organized and unorganized labor and the industrialist exactly in the situation that it is to-day. If there are strikes, that is a matter that would be handled by the agencies devoted to that purpose that are in the country at that time.[60]

Drafting 4,000,000 Men

The President, in the last war, had no difficulty whatsoever in obtaining men as they were needed. Congress cooperated with him to the fullest extent of its powers in passing the various draft acts and in granting him nearly

[60] *Ibid.*, pages 380–82.

unlimited authority through the medium of the Overman Act. There is absolutely no reason to believe that Congress, in the event of another war, will not cooperate in such manner again with the executive branch of the Government.

In the light of the geographical position of this country and the mechanical, chemical and bacteriological methods for carrying on war, which require a minimum contingent of man power, at least at the beginning of hostilities, the War Department's plan for the immediate mobilization of 4,000,000 men on the declaration of war is unnecessary. Furthermore, this precipitate withdrawal of 4,000,000 men from civilian activity is dangerous in that it may unnecessarily paralyze industry by stripping it of those needed in the transition stage between war and peace. In addition, it is not unlikely that, through malevolent manipulation, it might be used as an instrument for the destruction of the country's organized labor forces.

Compelling Labor

The United States Supreme Court in the Selective Draft Law Cases established the right of Congress to compel military service. The grant to Congress of power to raise and support armies, considered in conjunction with the grants of the powers to declare war, to make rules for the governing and regulation of the land and naval forces, and to make laws necessary and proper for executing the granted powers,[61] the Court held, includes the power to compel

[61] *See* Constitution of the United States, Art. I, sec. 8.

military service. This conclusion, the Court stated, is not only obvious upon the face of the Constitution but is also confirmed by an historical examination of the subject.

There would seem to be little doubt, therefore, that since Congress may compel one man to participate in armed conflict in war-time it may compel another to supply the instruments necessary to help carry out its declaration of war. To avoid confusion it is necessary that the country understand that Congress now has this war-time power.

In the light of this seemingly implied power it is especially important that the people are not misled by that part of the resolution which states that the Commission "shall not consider and shall not report upon the conscription of labor."[62] This prohibition, on its face, does not deny any implied power of Congress to draft labor. In other words, it does not mean that the Government lacks the power to conscript labor because this Commission was instructed not to consider the conscription of labor. It has that power. Whether it chooses to discuss or execute it is another matter.

Although the War Department at one time actively pushed a bill in the Senate for conscription of all man-power, labor and property, it does not at the present time propose to draft labor in war-time. This is evidenced by the statement made by General MacArthur to the Commission in which he drew a sharp distinction between working in a factory and serving in a trench. The General stated:

> Effective use of labor in industry, in war-time as in peace-time, can be had only through labor's voluntary cooperation.

[62] *See* above, page 12f.

Any system of forced labor, either by conscription or otherwise, could result only in failure. It would not be supported by public opinion and, even though tolerated by a people at war, the resentment of the workers on whom it was imposed would be a direct source of inefficient operation.[63]

Such is the present policy. It does not mean, however, that the War Department may not find it necessary to execute, through the President, the power of Congress under the Selective Draft Law Cases which inferentially gives Congress the right to draft men for any purpose necessary for carrying on a war.

Colonel Robbins, under questioning, gave the Commission an idea what sort of procedure would accompany such a gigantic mobilization when he recommended "the registration of civilians" in addition to the draft.

Mr. Collins—Going to another subject, you do not think that an amendment to the Constitution is necessary?

Colonel Robbins—No, sir.

Mr. Collins—To be recommended by this commission?

Colonel Robbins—No, sir.

Mr. Collins—Because you think that under existing law we can draft men for the Army and for any other purpose as we may need?

Colonel Robbins—I think the draft act has been repealed, Mr. Collins; I do not think it is in force.

Mr. Collins—But you say that Congress has the power?

Colonel Robbins—Yes, sir; to pass a draft act, and I think if they can pass a draft act calling men into the military service, they could pass a law for the registration of civilians. That is what I suggested.

63 War Policies Commission Hearings, page 374. *See* above, page 53f.

Mr. Collins—What do you mean?

Colonel Robbins—By the registration of civilians?

Mr. Collins—Yes.

Colonel Robbins—I think it would be a good thing.

Mr. Collins—That is so as to keep certain classes of labor from getting large salaries in the event of war?

Colonel Robbins—Well, to know where a man is and what he is doing.

Mr. Collins—So that you can put him to work?

Colonel Robbins—Put him to work.

Mr. Collins—That is all.[64]

Equalizing Burdens

The War Department, in its listed "conclusions concerning the problems facing this Commission," stated that:

The economic burdens must be equalized through:

(a) Systematic registration of wealth and all accretions thereto during the period of the emergency; and tax legislation framed to place an equitable burden thereon.

(b) Orderly and economic procurement by the Government itself under a comprehensive previously prepared plan similar to that herein described.

(c) Strong and intelligent leadership based on exact information and exercised through an organization adapted to the purpose and specially set up for the period of the emergency.

(d) Application of governmental controls to meet requirements of the specific situation and to prevent any profiteering at the national expense. These controls must include a priorities system and reasonable measures for the stabilization of prices.

(e) Prompt resumption of normal peace conditions upon the

[64] *Ibid.*, pages 260–61.

termination of the war. During the progress of any war the President should appoint a committee to study and prepare plans for demobilization. These plans must facilitate the re-employment of men returning to civil life from the Army and Navy and the freeing of industry of the accumulations of stocks produced to meet war requirements.[65]

At the end of the last war the Government sold a considerable quantity of its arms and munitions then in France to the Government of that country. The sales price of that material is now part of the French debt to the United States. It is probable that this procedure, carried out for "the freeing of industry of the accumulation of stocks produced to meet war requirements," merely aided "industry" at the expense of the entire United States citizenry. If the War Department contemplates a repetition of such action under similar conditions it is to be unequivocally condemned.

The War Department also desires Congress to grant it the funds for "educational orders." This type of order would permit the War Department to place contracts without complying with the legal necessity of inviting public bids. In effect, it really is a factory subsidy plan which would tend only to whet the appetite of the unscrupulous manufacturer whose desire for more profits is sharp enough without adding an additional stimulus in the form of legalized temptation.

The impossibility of preventing the abuse, on a huge scale, of educational orders was insisted upon by Mr. Collins in discussing this request with General MacArthur:

[65] *Ibid.*, pages 376–77.

Mr. Collins—Another recommendation of yours is with respect to educational orders. It is your idea that we ought to provide for educational orders now.

General MacArthur—It is. We submitted proposed legislation about that.

Mr. Collins—I know you did, but you really are doing that thing in another way under appropriations for experimentation, are you not?

General MacArthur—I know of no case myself where we have put in educational orders. We are anxious to get the legislation through.

Mr. Collins—You are spending that money for experimentation?

General MacArthur—Yes.

Mr. Collins—You would make your legislation fit all of the 4,000 articles you speak of?

General MacArthur—No; only those not of commercial manufacture.

Mr. Collins—What, for instance?

General MacArthur—What are some of the items that you are interested in?

Col. Irving J. Carr[66]—Antiaircraft firing equipment, range finders, and certain recuperators.

Mr. Collins—We are supplying those now.

Colonel Carr—We are manufacturing them in our own arsenals.

Mr. Collins—And don't you know that it would not be very long before you would have 25 or 30 other articles that manufacturers would want you to give educational orders for, and don't you know that it would be relatively a short time before some of the worst scandals would result that we have ever had in this country?

[66] Colonel Carr and Major General Moseley assisted General MacArthur on the stand.

General Moseley—You would control that by appropriations.
Mr. Collins—But you can not do it. . .[67]

It is astonishing that the War Department should have overlooked the Graham committee's recommendation, made after a thorough investigation of the widespread profiteering and corruption in war contracts, that the power of the Secretary of War "to suspend the requirements relating to advertising . . . be either entirely withdrawn or be definitely limited so as not to permit him to abrogate the wise public policy of taking competitive bids quickly by other means." In its report entitled "Expenditures in the War Department—Camps" the Select Committee on Expenditures in the War Department, on April 10, 1920, emphatically stated:

> Your committee respectfully recommends that the power of the Secretary of War to suspend the requirements relating to advertising, under section 3709 and the amendatory sections, be either entirely withdrawn or be definitely limited so as not to permit him to abrogate the wise public policy of taking competitive bids quickly by other means. Your committee respectfully recommends that such legislation be made broad enough to cover other officers now having similar powers of suspension.[68]

The War Department in "Recommendations" relative to the adoption by Congress of "a like joint resolution . . . which will make public announcement to the Nation of the policies set forth" in its General Mobilization Plan, states that certain salutary conditions will result. It be-

[67] War Policies Commission Hearings, page 384.
[68] *Op. cit.*, page 145.

lieves "that the announcement of these principles as approved policies of the Government will—"

(B) Facilitate the successful conduct of war, and effect a just and equitable distribution of war's economic burdens and, as far as practicable, of its human burdens, when once it has been deliberately undertaken.[69]

No reasonable being can reconcile the payment to industry of a 6 per cent profit based "on what it is claimed is the investment"—even assuming that it is possible for a Government such as ours to so supervise private industry as to keep it reasonably within this figure—with the meager payment made to the soldier and with the latter's great difficulties in the inevitable period of economic readjustment. If that is "a just and equitable distribution of war's economic burdens" then words have lost their meaning and justice has been removed further away from the reach of the common man than ever before.

The listing of war's "human burdens" after the "economic burdens" is indeed a very sad commentary on our present civilization. It also illuminates the War Department's mental outlook.

Besides effecting "a just and equitable distribution of war's economic burdens," by a complex price and profit arrangement for industry, the War Department desires the same sort of distribution "as far as practicable, of its human burdens." Its desire to do this, however, ends with the mere statement of intention—"and as far as practicable, of its human burdens." This very statement partakes of

[69] War Policies Commission Hearings, page 377.

cruelty when bracketed with a commercial plan designed to afford, in the words of Major Wilkes of the War Department,[70] "free negotiation between the buyer and seller."

It seems inconceivable that people should still be discussing "equalizing the burdens of war" after the horrendous experiences of the world conflict, after a flowing of blood which even the medieval poets never imagined. This seeming forgetfulness makes it necessary to restate that stark truth: it is impossible to equalize the human burdens of war. To qualify any intention to do so with an "as far as practicable" is not only evasive but cruel as well. Is it suggested that it is possible to compensate a human being for loss of life, limb or mental peacefulness by those who have the power, potential or otherwise, to tear a human being from a peaceful existence and cast him into a hell of lung-blistering gas and literal fire?

All of this does not mean, however, that the Government's program should end with lip service to the impossibility of rendering the soldier some substitute for compensation. On this point, a decent program, though truly a negative one, could be adopted. In the event of war Congress should at least take measures to see to it that no member of society, no financier, no manufacturer, no general, for instance, should be permitted to live on a physical plane one iota above that of the common soldier as far as it is humanly possible to bring the civilian and military scales of living into line.

In the event of war the Government will no doubt take

[70] *Ibid.*, page 386.

over the railroads, just as it did in the last war. Through this control of transportation it virtually dictated the kind and amount of food the civilian population consumed. It will no doubt do this again if necessary. By a rigidly supervised system of food transportation and distribution, interference with which would be a serious military offense, the Government could so control the food supply that the gap between the common soldier and the civilian would be as small as possible. It is true that this proposal presents great difficulties since homes, except under conditions of invasion or proximity to the theatre of war, are not needed by the military. Nevertheless, by a proper registration of private homes, the families therein, the number of people in each family, and so on, the Government can see to it that such essential workers as those who labor in munition factories and related industries have the necessary, proper and adequate housing. This, in addition to affording the soldier some spiritual consolation, will militate towards securing more physical comforts than would otherwise be the case were only sympathy and speeches contributed.

Whom Does the War Department Protect?

There is nothing in General MacArthur's plan which will prevent a repetition of the widespread profiteering of the last war. It will not "remove the profits of war." It will not even minimize the profits of war. In reality, it offers an incentive to certain anti-social business organizations to whose interest it will be to exert their power and influence to provoke a war.

Concerning equalizing the burdens of war, even "as far as practicable," when the War Department proposes to pay industry a profit of 6 per cent in war-time, it is in effect favoring one class of society, already the most powerful, at the expense of all the others. Failure to give more practical recognition to the essential justice of treating all classes alike, wherever and whenever possible, shows an inexcusable and lamentable lack of courage. It is a failure to realize that the War Department exists to serve the whole people. Finally, it is tangible proof that the War Department merits the charge of being the ally of a social-industrial-financial caste. In this role it is a danger to the general interests of the great body of citizens over whose lives it wields formidable authority.

The following excerpts from the War Department's very original treatise, "Citizenship," Training Manual Number 2000-25, indicates its social philosophy:

> *Dangers to representative government:* Whenever the republican form of government has not achieved success the difficulty has not been with the system but with its faulty application.
>
> Several dangerous experiments have been proposed, such as the initiative, referendum, recall, and the election of judges. Departures from constitutional principles threaten to impair the efficiency of our representative form of government, and if continued, will ultimately destroy it. (Page 99.)
>
> *Democracy:* A government of the masses.
>
> Authority derived through mass meeting or any other form of "direct" expression.
>
> Results in mobocracy.

Attitude toward property is communistic—negating property rights.

Attitude toward law is that the will of the majority shall regulate, whether it be based upon deliberation or governed by passion, prejudice, and impulse, without restraint or regard to consequences.

Results in demagogism, license, agitation, discontent, anarchy. (Page 91.)

Our Government is the most nearly perfect of all in securing individual rights and insuring the blessings of liberty. In no other nation is equal opportunity and equal protection assured, with such equal division of reward for labor and services rendered. (Page 88.)

There is more and greater work to be done with each succeeding generation. The achievements of individuals in the past are a challenge to the youth of today. There are still further fields of exploration, adventure, and accomplishment, and a multitude of past achievements to be perfected. Every man possessed of the will to work finds his opportunity awaiting him. (Page 71.)

Labor advancement: During the World War the wage earner learned to put his excess money into Liberty bonds. He caught the idea of investment, acquired the habit of systematic saving, discovered the strength that lies in consolidating the small savings of the many. He began to understand the meaning of capital, lost his fear of it, and found a way to have a part in its benefits. (Page 61.)

Under no other government are property rights of the individual so provided with safeguards for their full protection. Property is at the base of civilization. Without incentive of right to its private possession and full protection against confiscation no progress would be made in material betterment.

Economic liberty, the power of initiative, and the protection of property rights have developed a philosophy of life peculiar to America—the "dignity of work." Every American is expected to be a worker.

Based upon the constitutional assurance of the security of property, finance and labor have joined in the creation of industry, making America the richest nation in the world. Her wealth has been distributed to the enrichment of her entire population. (Page 79.)

The only aristocracy that America will ever recognize is that of "brains"—"the tools to him who can handle them." The tribute in honor and the reward in wealth accorded to brains in this land of opportunity are not equaled in any other country. Brains ask for no "equality of condition," want only "equality of opportunity." (Page 69.)

This is the land of "equality of opportunity." The citizen alone can determine the measure of his participation in freedom's field. What he does and how he does it will be dependent upon his will to work, the thoroughness of his education, and the quality of his ideals. (Page 72.)

Through equality of opportunity America gives each individual citizen an equal chance, yet his ability, intelligence, and character distinguish and classify him as progress is made. (Page 103.)

The United States has acquired a clear title to every square inch of land which has been added to that of the original thirteen Colonies. All territory annexed to the United States since 1803 has been acquired either by treaty or purchase, except Texas and Hawaii, which were admitted to the Union by their own request. In the latter instance, however, $200,000 was paid as a compensation to Liliuokalani. (Page 112.)

The *ex cathedra* pronouncements on "equality of opportunity" and the distribution of wealth in America "to the enrichment of her entire population" should prove distinctly revealing to the 10,000,000 unemployed.

CHAPTER FOUR

"AGREEMENTS" BETWEEN THE WAR DEPARTMENT AND INDUSTRY

What may be expected from any profit arrangement in war-time between the War Department and "the representatives of industry" is shown by the Graham committee's revelation of the diabolic disregard for life and criminal absence of social consciousness that corroded nearly every cog of the War Department–Industrial organization during the last war.

Food

In the Graham committee's report made to the House of Representatives on July 28, 1919, "relating to the War Department's nonactivities in the sale of the very large quantities of food supplies now held in storage in the United States," the War Department was reprimanded for entering into an agreement with the canners' association whereby 200,000,000 cans of vegetables—paid for by the people—were kept off the domestic market "to protect the canners who had sold the produce, from competition with the governmental surplus."

Airplanes

Although the Government spent over $1,000,000,000 for aviation up to June 30, 1919, not one American-built pursuit or combat plane or one American-built bombing plane reached the front. The only airplanes constructed in this country, which reached France, were two hundred and thirteen DeHaviland 4s, one thousand nine hundred and thirty-seven of which were produced in October, 1918, alone, at a cost of from $10,000,000 to $15,000,000. This type of plane, mainly responsible for the terribly high rate of American aviation fatalities—General Menoher, the then Chief of Air Service, stated that the battle fatalities for hours flown were three times as great for American aviators as for either the British or Belgian—was "criminally constructed," according to Captain Eddie Rickenbacker in his testimony before the Graham aviation committee.

Captain Rickenbacker informed the Graham committee:

> From every side Fokkers were piquing upon the clumsy Liberty machines (DH-4's) which, with their criminally constructed fuel tanks, offered so easy a target to the incendiary bullets of the enemy that their unfortunate pilots called this boasted achievement of our Aviation Department their "flaming coffins." During that one brief flight over Grand Pre I saw three of these crude machines go down in flames, an American pilot and an American gunner in each "flaming coffin," dying this frightful and needless death.[71]

The Senate investigation of the monumental negligence and corruption in airplane manufacturing revealed that the authorities for whose direct use the huge expenditure was being made were apparently ignorant of the domestic plans.

[71] Graham committee report on "Expenditures in the War Department —Aviation," *op. cit.*, page 10.

General Pershing, the head of the American Expeditionary Force, knew "very little of the construction program in America nor the reasons why we had no further planes."

Testimony, October 31, 1919, before the Joint Military Committee briefly gives the story of America's aviation record from a witness of acknowledged authority:

Senator Chamberlain—Did you at any time have enough planes of any make of American or foreign to train that body [aviators then in France]?

Gen. Pershing—No; we were always short.

Senator Chamberlain—In other words, we had a body of young men over there to be trained that could not be trained because we did not have the facilities to train them.

Gen. Pershing—Yes, sir. That is true.

* * * * *

Mr. James—How many American fighting planes were there in France at the signing of the armistice?

Gen. Pershing—None. We had the DeHaviland 4s.

* * * * *

Mr. Miller—I mean combat planes.

Gen. Pershing—No combat planes.

* * * * *

Mr. Kearns—Do you know the reason why there were no other American-made planes over there?

Gen. Pershing—I know very little of the construction program in America nor the reasons why we had no further planes. The only reason that I can give is that there were no planes ready to ship.

Bearing on the same question Col. Patrick, Chief of Air Service, A.E.F., in August, 1918, testified: . . .

Mr. Frear—So we were woefully weak in our own Air Service, both in machines and men?
Col. Patrick—Yes, sir.

Our utter failure to produce fighting planes after 19 months of war is disclosed by one question:

Mr. Magee—As far as the manufacture of pursuit planes or bombing planes in the United States is concerned, we are practically in the same position (August, 1919) we were in when we entered the World War?
Col. Patrick—Quite true.[72]

Under the heading "Responsibility Fixed for Use of 'Utterly Unsafe' Planes" the Graham committee reported:

In spite of wanton waste of lives, these DH-4's, the only American-made planes that reached the front, were kept in production after their dangerous and clumsy construction was a matter of common knowledge. The last Director of Aircraft, Mr. John D. Ryan,[73] just prior to his long European trip with Secretary Baker in August, 1918, testified before the Thomas Senate subcommittee a few weeks after he had canceled the order for the utterly useless Bristol that could not carry the Liberty motor. The following testimony is from Director Ryan on the DH-4. His responsibility for aviation and needless waste of life was then being weighed by that committee:

Senator Reed—You know that the best and most experienced flyers, a number of them in this country, have testified before this committee that they regard the DeHaviland machine as utterly unsafe and that they would refuse to go up in it or send subordinates up in it?

[72] *Ibid.*, pages 2–3.

[73] Who's Who, 1930–31, lists Mr. Ryan as chairman of the Board of Directors of the Anaconda Copper Mining Company.

Mr. Ryan—I understand that some have testified that they have refused to go up in it or let subordinates go up in it.

Senator Reed—You propose to go on making the DeHaviland 4 machines?

Mr. Ryan—Until we can put the DeHaviland 9 in production.

Senator Reed—Do you intend to do that regardless of any testimony that may be given by experienced flyers that the machine is utterly unsafe?

Mr. Ryan—I am not convinced that the burden of testimony of the flyers throughout the country is that the DeHaviland 4 is an unsafe machine.

This testimony is taken from the official record of the Thomas Senate Committee hearings to show the purpose of responsible American aircraft production officials from Squier and Deeds, at the beginning, and down to Ryan at the finish, to keep manufacturing for use of American aviators the "utterly unsafe" DH-4. Equal responsibility rests with the head of the War Department who was informed of the facts—for Secretary Baker, who approved the Squier program at the outset, was before the Thomas committee in August, 1918, when the following startling statement was made to him by a Senator of that committee:

Senator New—It is a fact that every flyer that we have had before this committee as a witness, including several who have seen long service abroad, both with our own forces, the British forces, and the French forces, have testified that the DeHaviland 4 machine, with the defects appearing in it as it has been produced at the Dayton-Wright factory, is highly dangerous and ought not under any circumstances be used; and at least one officer has testified that he would no longer send men up from his field in a machine of that type until after these defects had been remedied. In view of that condition, as it has been expressed and recorded by the men who are best qualified to pass upon the conditions and quality of that machine, I at least think that it was a very great error of policy and judgment to have sent them forward before these mistakes were corrected, and I wanted to know whether or not you agreed with that view.

Mr. Baker—The subcommittee, of course, has a great advantage over me in that I have not been permitted to see any of the testimony the committee has taken, so that I do not know anything about this concurrence of opinion to which you refer.

Senator New—I am telling you now what that opinion is.

More specifically, Secretary Baker testified before our own committee, July 31, 1919, as follows:

Secretary Baker—Mr. Ryan and I talked over the general question . . . and I approved that we should not suspend making any machine we were then making, but we should go on and make it and get ready to make others.

This was Mr. Baker's judgment when the only machine apart from training planes then or thereafter produced by the United States was the "utterly unsafe" DH-4 plane.

Secretary Baker and Mr. Ryan, his appointee, were both faced by the Senate committee with these facts, which were pressed upon them when they sailed together for Europe in August, 1918, at which time Mr. Ryan declared to Senator Reed that he proposed to go on making the dangerous DH-4's.[74]

President Wilson, early in 1918, commissioned Charles Evans Hughes to investigate the aviation situation. The Senate Committee on Military Affairs entered the situation

[74] Graham committee report on "Expenditures in the War Department —Aviation," *op. cit.,* pages 11-12.

by the appointment of a subcommittee to investigate the evidences of aircraft corruption and inefficiency. The Graham committee, in regard to these two aviation investigations, both of which it approved, said:

> The Hughes report fixed responsibility on certain officials, from Gen. Squier and Deeds down to subordinate officers, and recited failures in measuring up to requirements. The Thomas Senate committee report devoted brief consideration to individual inefficiency, but pointed out the disastrous policy pursued in sacrificing everything and subordinating all energies to perfecting the Liberty motor.
>
> In the judgment of this committee both the Hughes report and the Thomas report reached correct conclusions, and it is not necessary to reiterate those conclusions; but responsibility for failures should be chargeable to those at the top who permitted inefficiency and stupidity to govern what ought to have been a vigorous branch of our military program . . .
>
> ### Official Responsibility for Aviation Failures
>
> . . . Justice Hughes' report says of Gen. Squier:
>
> > The duty of providing an adequate organization for aircraft production was left to the Signal Corps. It is quite clear that this undertaking was beyond the competency of the Chief Signal Officer.
>
> This reckless, foolish policy threw aside every tried life preserver, every efficient air weapon used by all other countries after 30 months of war, and resulted in disastrous blunders and inexcusable delays, when delays meant unnecessary loss of life and possible loss of battles. Gen. Squier threw the die in April, 1917, and pooled everything for the Liberty motor

experiment, which was used in the hopeless DH-4s, ignoring all other weapons.

Secretary of War Baker, while before our committee, said he approved Gen. Squier's course when he responded, "That was my judgment at the time and still is my judgment."

On Secretary Baker's shoulders must rest equal responsibility for failure to procure other engines and other planes when pooling all energies in the Liberty motor. Thousands of workmen were idle in airplane factories waiting for work, while Europe shouted for planes. Gen. Squier was finally relieved from active production about the time he testified before the Senate committee after nine months of valuable time had been wasted. All energies continued to be bent in building the useless DH-4, as shown by Director Ryan's testimony previously cited, and the same disastrous policy was thereafter pursued to the end of the war and approved by Secretary Baker.

It is not the province of this committee to declare the measure of responsibility of any official, but we would be derelict in duty if we failed to present to the House what we believe to be the causes for America's aviation failure and the resulting lack of confidence in any present War Department aviation plans.

Official responsibility reaches back prior to the war when Congress created a Council of National Defense, August 29, 1916. An active, virile organization that would insure ample protection to the country in time of peace and full preparation if our country became involved in war was needed. Over six months elapsed, while "Rome was burning," before the council was finally organized on March 3, 1917, with Secretary of War Baker as chairman. Gen. Squier, then Chief Signal Officer, was in control of aircraft matters. Nothing had been done in aviation—nothing was likely to be done. He pooled everything on the Liberty motor when he did start, after the war was on, and put all the Nation's aviation program eggs in one basket.

Responsibility for Deeds

Col. Edward A. Deeds, of Dayton, Ohio, was placed in charge of the Equipment Division of Aviation under Gen. Squier in August, 1917, four months after our entry into the war. Nothing appears in any of the hearings of any investigation to show why Deeds was appointed. Deeds knew nothing of aircraft. Deeds had never been connected with any Government activity. Secretary Baker says he never saw Deeds until after his appointment, although Deeds and Secretary Baker were both from Ohio.

Justice Hughes' report found that Deeds began his activities by centering aircraft operations at Dayton, Ohio; that he gave large contracts to his business associates—Kettering, Talbott, and others in that city, although they had no previous experience in such matters; that he located several aviation fields around Dayton in improper locations, and also located fields in Florida without authority or explanation; that Deeds was largely interested in corporations controlling the Delco ignition system used in the projected Liberty motor, whereas prior to its use on the Liberty, the magneto system had been used on all airplane engines.

The following is from the Hughes report:

At the inception of the Government's aviation activity in connection with the war and within the sphere of Col. Deeds' important if not commanding influence, his former business associates were placed at once, through Government contracts, in a position where they had assurance of very large profits upon a comparatively small investment of their own money, and in addition were able to secure generous salaries which they charged against the Government as part of the cost of manufacture.

After reciting evidence in support of this conclusion, Justice Hughes finds:

The evidence with respect to Col. Edward A. Deeds should be presented to the Secretary of War, to the end that Col. Deeds may be tried by court-martial under articles 95 and 96 of the Articles of War.

Justice Hughes' report in part 2 of this report includes a detailed statement of testimony on which the finding was based.

In the Attorney General's report this finding appears:

I acquiesce in the recommendations of Judge Hughes that the facts be submitted to the Secretary of War.

Because of these findings and recommendations for court-martial it is proper to say that about four years before his appointment to produce aircraft, Deeds achieved considerable notoriety in Ohio, where he was prosecuted in the Federal court for alleged bribery and criminal methods in driving his competitors out of the cash register business and was convicted by a jury after a trial lasting over a month and sentenced to imprisonment for one year.

An appeal was taken, with 50 assignments of error, and the case was reversed and no retrial was ever had. Deeds' innocence may be conceded, for the sake of argument, though no second trial occurred, but the charge, conviction, and court record were enough to put any responsible official on inquiry before giving Deeds a place of transcendent importance in charge of matters about which he knew nothing.

Why Was Deeds' Court-Martial Prevented?

For Deeds' alleged efforts to place large Government contracts with his business associates in Dayton, under questionable arrangements, and for other reasons stated in his report,

Justice Hughes recommended Deeds for court-martial, and Attorney General Gregory joined in the report to the extent of declaring Col. Deeds' conduct inexcusable, reprehensible, and censurable, and recommended that all the facts be submitted to the Secretary of War.

Based on the Hughes record, the Judge Advocate General's office on November 11, 1918, submitted its report approving the Hughes recommendations and holding, in addition, that if Col. Deeds was under oath when testifying before the Senate committee he should be court-martialed for perjury, if false statements were shown to have been made.

Subsequently, Secretary of War Baker sent word to the Judge Advocate General's office requesting that other witnesses be heard on behalf of Deeds and that the report be reconsidered. This action, your committee is informed, was unprecedented. Col. Deeds' attorney and two business associates, connected with these same Government contracts, were thereupon heard and a new report rendered exonerating Deeds. Secretary Baker's activity in protecting Deeds against Justice Hughes' finding is at once astonishing and significant. With a record that affected lives of men and charges of inordinate selfishness supported by specific facts, Deeds should have been placed on trial to be convicted if guilty, to be vindicated if innocent. According to the testimony, Secretary Baker prevented such action.

Col. Deeds was thereafter banqueted in Washington and praised by Gen. Squier for his record in aircraft production.

The approval of Deeds by Squier and the saving of Deeds from court-martial by Secretary Baker require no further discussion to reveal disheartening conditions surrounding American aircraft production in 1917. Whether conditions ever improved is a matter of grave doubt. Gen. Squier is still Chief Signal Officer and Gen. Menoher is now in charge of aviation —an Artillery officer, courteous and obliging, but without aviation training or experience. Secretary Baker's judgment is a matter of record.

Deeds, after filling many positions in the Aircraft production branch of the Signal Corps, was finally sidetracked about January, 1918, and Col. Robert L. Montgomery, a bond dealer, was placed at the head of the Equipment Division, "but despite the change in technical relation it is apparent that Col. Deeds remained in practical charge, under the Chief Signal Officer, of production."
(Hughes' report.)

Potter and Ryan, Directors

. . . In an official War Department publication, published by Maj. Mixter, on "Aircraft production facts," appears the following:

In January, 1918, W. C. Potter, of the Guggenheim interests, became Chief of the Equipment Division. When the Air Service was separated from the Signal Corps in May, 1918, John D. Ryan, of the Anaconda Copper Co., was appointed Director of Aircraft Production and later an Assistant Secretary of War and Director of Air Service. Mr. Potter continued as First Assistant Director of the Bureau of Aircraft Production . . .

Deeds, Potter, and Ryan Without Any Knowledge of Aircraft

Deeds had no knowledge of aircraft nor have any known reasons ever been given for his appointment. Equally inscrutable are reasons for appointment by Secretary Baker of either Potter or Ryan to their positions of great aircraft responsibility. Testifying before the Thomas Senate committee, Director Ryan was asked:

Senator Reed—What was Mr. Potter's occupation or business before he came in?

Mr. Ryan—He was in the mining and metallurgical business and connected with the Guggenheims.

Senator Reed—And never had anything to do with aircraft?

Mr. Ryan—I think not.

That briefly presents Potter's aircraft qualifications.

Testifying before the same Thomas Senate committee, Director Ryan was asked regarding Potter, Kellogg, Wolff, Brown, Fletcher, Downey, Lockhart, Mixter, and Leadbetter, all of whom were his assistants in aircraft production:

Senator Reed—There was not a single one of these men who had had experience so far as you know in aircraft production?

Mr. Ryan—Not so far as I know.

Senator Reed—They were men that you think had the final say in regard to contracts before you took charge?

Mr. Ryan—Subject, of course, to Gen. Squier, who was Chief of the Signal Corps. They were under him.[75]

Copper

Every member of the cooperative committee on copper appointed to assist the Council of National Defense Advisory Commission under Chairman Bernard M. Baruch, banker, according to the Graham investigating committee's report, "was deeply interested in the copper industry and in the success of various properties owned or controlled in part by them." The cooperative committee on copper, appointed by Mr. Baruch, consisted of: John D. Ryan of

[75] *Ibid.*, pages 17–21.

the Anaconda Copper Mining Company; R. L. Agassiz; W. A. Clark of the United Verde Mining Company and the Magma Copper Company; Murry M. Guggenheim, an officer and stockholder of the Chile Copper Company and heavily interested in the huge Guggenheim copper interests; James McLean, Vice-President of the Phelps-Dodge Corporation and a director in the Greene-Cananea Company; Charles MacNeill, President of the Utah Copper Company; and Stephen Birch, who was stated in the Graham hearings to be possessed of various copper holdings.

This was the committee, says the Graham report, "whose function it was to assist in or advise as to the purchase of copper for the Government." In short, this cooperative committee of copper producers, through a sales agency called the United Metal Selling Company, with Government authority "practically controlled the companies that in turn controlled the price of copper in the United States." It is obvious that the tax-payers were at their mercy.

In the matter of the production of copper, as in all other industries and trades, the various cooperative committees who were appointed were selected, not by the Government, but by the respective trades and interests, and, as naturally would be expected, these gentlemen had in mind the condition of their various trades and were supposed and expected to represent them in their various transactions with the Government. On the other hand, on the part of the Government, there was no one who knew anything about the various trades or interests involved, excepting in the most casual and fragmentary way, and this condition continued to a very considerable extent throughout the entire war and certainly throughout the war so far as the purchases of copper were concerned.[76]

All those copper producers not yet represented at this stage, early in 1917, were brought into the picture by Mr. Baruch's appointment of Eugene Meyer, Jr., as his representative in the arrangement of a copper producers' committee. Mr. Meyer, in the words of the Graham committee, "at that time, had large copper investments and was heavily interested in the business."

The companies represented in this copper combine did not fail to make the best of their opportunities.

The Utah Copper Co. in 1917 made a profit of $32,000,000, which was 200 per cent of its capital stock, and in 1918 a profit of $24,750,000, which was 150 per cent of its capital stock. The Calumet & Hecla Mining Co. in 1917 made a profit of $9,500,000, or 800 per cent of its capital stock, and in 1918, $3,500,000, or 300 per cent of its capital stock. The Inspiration Consolidated Copper Co. in 1917 made a profit of $12,260,000, or 55 per cent of its capital stock, and in 1918, $9,250,000, or 40 per cent of its capital stock. The Kennecott Copper Co. in 1917 made a profit of $11,826,000, or 70 per cent of its capital stock, and in 1918, $9,390,135.90, or 60 per cent of its capital stock. It is probable that other companies in the list made similar profits, but the exact information is not available without a careful and detailed audit of the books of these various companies.

The profits given here are net.[77]

The conclusion of the Graham committee on the copper

[76] Graham committee report on "Expenditures in the Ordnance Department," 66th Cong., 3rd Ses., Report No. 1400, pages 86–87.

[77] *Ibid.*, page 94.

producers obviates the necessity for prolonging the record of the profiteering rampant in this industry during the war.

A fair and candid résumé of the whole situation can not fail to convince the reader that the arrangement thus entered into was one extremely favorable to at least a few of the copper producers, and that from this arrangement, and because of the necessity and demands of the Government during the war, those who operated these copper-producing properties were enabled to make and did make extravagant and extraordinary profits.[78]

Instances of corruption and profiteering in other basic industries operated by "patriotic industrialists" could easily be cited. It is not necessary to do so. The extent of the astounding corruption is little appreciated and generally ignored. Nevertheless, we can and must take these matters into consideration in preparing any peace-time or war-time plans which would necessarily have to consider the utilization of the country's resources.

If this is to be done it will first be necessary to convert those who hold an opinion similar to that of Mr. Baker, former Secretary of War. In spite of the facts brought out by the Graham committee, Mr. Baker, in answer to the question ". . . can you give us any thought on how to prosecute a war, or would you prosecute the next one just like we did the last one?" is of the opinion that the "enterprise" was "successful."

Of course, there is always a tendency on the part of a man who has had part in one successful enterprise to want to repeat

[78] *Ibid.*, page 95.

his success and to think it was done just right the time before and to want to do it the next time in the same way. That is a natural human tendency, I suppose . . .

Chairman Graham, in that section of the Committee's report dealing with enforcing the law against war profiteers, disagreed rather sharply with the conclusions of Mr. Baker concerning the "success" of the "enterprise." He said:

How many criminals have been uncovered? It matters not how many have been uncovered, it goes without saying that none will be prosecuted. . . . During the war hundreds of people were prosecuted by the vigilant Attorney General for violation of the espionage act, but who has heard of a prosecution of a war profiteer? I say to you, with a full comprehension of the nature of the charge, that there are thousands of men who have violated the law during the war, of whom the Attorney General's Department has full knowledge, and none of whom has been or will be prosecuted. You talk of prosecution. You might as well submit to the prisoner in the dock the question of his own guilt. There will be no prosecution, no courts-martial. What this committee uncovers will be laughed to scorn by the War Department and Department of Justice.[79]

[79] As quoted in the War Policies Commission Hearings, page 614.

CHAPTER FIVE

A WOLF AND SOME LAMBS TESTIFY

The line of cleavage between the dominant element of the Commission represented by Secretary of War Hurley and that represented by Representative Ross A. Collins of Mississippi, whose faction consisted of himself, was drawn early. The Mississippi Congressman was impolitic enough to remember that "to promote peace" was written in the sub-head of the resolution ostensibly for some tangible purpose. His error was sharply brought to his attention on the first day of the hearings during the first secret session of the Commission when Representative Hadley of Washington proposed that Mr. Collins' remarks be expunged from the record, or, failing that, that they be not transcribed in the record. Representative Collins was wise enough to call the bluff. "Gentlemen, put that resolution in writing and then I'll resign." They saw the light, apparently visualizing newspaper headlines proclaiming the attempted censorship. From then on it was, as the testimony graphically shows, Mr. Hurley, Secretary of War, against Mr. Collins of Mississippi, then the ranking Democratic member of the House Subcommittee on War Department Appropriations, and now its chairman.

Throughout the hearings most of the old saws were recited—the best preparation for peace is to be prepared for war, America has never declared war contrary to the will of the people, we will go to war only to defend ourselves, ad infinitum. The bankers, financiers, industrialists, railroad men, army and naval officers, congressmen, ex-congressmen, ex-editors, ex-cabinet members, and other celebrities, all came before the Commission like heads on a moving belt—and with one or two exceptions all answered they were ready to serve, ready at a reasonable return, that is, for "just compensation."[80] Under his plan, said Mr. Baruch, in forty-eight hours, "we could get an organization of men here . . . that would get this [the plan] into smooth working order inside of two weeks."

Just a short distance away, in the State Department building facing the south grounds of the White House, officials were solemnly preparing for the 1932 Geneva Disarmament Conference.

The Lambs

The line of cleavage between the theoretical and the practicing peace organizations was as sharp and clear as that between Secretary of War Hurley, who described himself as "a peace advocate"[81] and Representative Collins who has always disclaimed the status of pacifist.[82]

[80] In treating hearings which consumed several months' time and eight hundred printed pages I regret to say that I was forced to forego the discussion of a few witnesses and proposals—whose mention I did not consider indispensable to this study—so as not to lose sight of the main issues involved.

[81] War Policies Commission Hearings, page 768.

[82] In a speech before the House of Representatives on February 19, 1932,

Benjamin Marsh, executive secretary of the People's Lobby—Professor John Dewey is its president—proposed the calling of an "international economic disarmament conference" which would have as its main purpose the reconciliation of conflicting economic forces.

"Several measures of international cooperation are essential to convince the world how stupid war is," he said, "but the following are of immediate importance:"

Greater freedom in the exchange of goods between nations.

A public record of terms, and conditions under which obtained, of concessions held by foreigners in every undeveloped nation to be deposited with some international agency such as the League of Nations.

Determination by some agreement between international investment bankers or by some agency of the League of Nations of procedure they will apply with respect to private loans to

Mr. Collins advocated the adoption of the use of gas as an efficient and comparatively humane instrument of war. He said:

> The advantages of chemical warfare in the defense of the United States should not be overlooked. . . .
>
> Chemical warfare does not bring about material damage. Gas is spread throughout the area, which during the existence of such gas is uninhabitable. But after a comparatively short period, normal economic life may continue at the point where it ceased previous to the conflict. . . .
>
> Chemical warfare is economical in the positive as well as the negative sense. The more efficient the chemical branch of the defense service the less expenditure is required for some other branches. . . . The mass formations of the past war have gone forever. No longer in the face of modern methods of warfare and the mechanized army can mere troops take any, except a very dependent part, in any future conflict. This country would do well to decrease its personnel, not merely so as to eliminate its military minded groups but in the interest of efficiency. . . . Personnel, therefore, must diminish in favor of material. . . . (*Congressional Record,* Feb. 19, 1932, pages 4493–94.)

undeveloped nations and citizens thereof, and for collection of debts, and agreement of governments not to approve nor influence the making of such, or any other loans by their nationals, similar to the resolution recently adopted on this subject by the Senate of the United States.

Adoption of some plan for the international allocation of natural resources and other raw materials similar to the system in operation among the Allies for the World War period.

Mutual concessions as to reparations and interallied debts and recognition that world peace will be in unstable equilibrium as long as America has about two-fifths of the world's income in wealth but continues its policy of extending its influences and increasing its wealth and income at the expense of nations less efficient and less lavishly endowed by nature with natural resources.

Adherence, without abdication of essential rights, to the World Court.[83]

After a lengthy colloquy on Mr. Marsh's stand that the problem of war is an economic problem which can be solved only by improved national and international conditions, Mr. Hurley made the gesture of asking him to name names:

Secretary Hurley— . . . Do you know of anyone who wants war?

Mr. Marsh—I have said that I think anybody who advocates a system which leads to it.

Secretary Hurley—Well, who advocates it? Now, tell me some person, in your opinion, who wants war who is charged with any responsibility in connection with this matter. Name him.

Mr. Marsh—Who maintains the marines in Nicaragua?

[83] War Policies Commission Hearings, page 324.

Secretary Hurley—Well, I have asked you—you have made the assertion about some one wanting war, and I have asked you who. You make the general statement, and I have asked you to name some one.

Mr. Marsh—Why, anyone who maintains conditions which lead to war I think can be fairly said to want war—not active aggressive war right off, but they want to maintain that system, if war commences, where they would be ready for it. As I remember, Mr. Coolidge said, "Where the American dollar is, there is American territory." I think I am quoting him correctly.

Secretary Hurley—Let me get down to names: Are you saying ex-President Coolidge wants war?

Mr. Marsh—I think any man who takes a position like that would be in serious danger of having his remarks so interpreted and should take such responsibility for his remarks.[84]

In answer to a request for a suggestion to help the Commission in its work, Mr. Marsh replied:

I would have the Government take over every dollar, every factory, every person in case of war, and equalize the pay according to the cost of living in the cities, and let them know you are going to do it, and pay for the war as you go, as we tried to get them to do in the last war. That would help. It would not, of course, equalize it; but, as I have made clear, you can not equalize human beings and money; it can not be done.[85]

When Mr. Marsh had the temerity to point out the danger to a country of a strongly entrenched military caste the Secretary of War hurled such intellectual thunderbolts

[84] *Ibid.*, page 328.
[85] *Ibid.*, page 332.

as—Do you think that the Government of the United States is worthy of being maintained and perpetuated? Are you in favor of the administration of justice through the judiciary? Do you approve of the judicial system of the United States? Are you a Socialist? A Bolshevist?

Secretary Hurley— . . . Do you think that the Government of the United States is worthy of being maintained and perpetuated?

Mr. Marsh—I think the people of the United States are worthy of being maintained and perpetuated. Governments may come and governments may go.

Secretary Hurley—I did not ask you that question.

Mr. Marsh—Governments may come and governments may go.

Secretary Hurley—Just wait a minute. We ought to get together. I did not ask you anything about perpetuating the people of the United States. I assume that will be done. I asked you this question: Do you believe that the Government of the United States is worthy of maintenance and of perpetuation?

Mr. Marsh—If you mean the Hoover administration, heavens knows I do not, and I am perfectly willing to make that clear, But if you mean to say whether we want to have the form of government—

Secretary Hurley—I do not mean a word except what I have said, and you have dodged the question four different times. Do you feel that the Government of these United States is worthy of maintenance and perpetuation? Now, that is clear English.

Mr. Marsh—It is worthy of maintenance and perpetuation, and badly needs improvement, so that it will be out of the control of the big interests that now own it, in my judgment. But the Government will go on, I sincerely hope, and I doubt if you are going to need an army to maintain it. Now, there was pending before this Congress—

Secretary Hurley—By what means would you maintain the Government in time of emergency?

Mr. Marsh—In times of emergency?

Secretary Hurley—Yes.

Mr. Marsh—For one thing, by looking after the people who are starving, which the last Congress would not do, although we begged them to, and not relying upon the Red Cross or any other subterfuges for the Government, which I think should be perpetuated and made to do its duty in regard to its own people. I am not against the Government; I am always for gradual changes—sometimes they have to be rapid—by peaceful methods. But as to whether the Government has changed a good deal, every amendment to the Constitution, if I correctly understand it, involves some change in the form of government. . . .[86]

Mr. Marsh also committed the heresy of suggesting the elimination in war-time of the "institution of private profit."

Mr. Marsh— . . . As I stated, if you get into war, the only way, in any way whatsoever, to equalize it, is to do away with the institution of private profit in land and in all other agencies of production. That won't equalize human beings and the wealth idea; but as between wealth and the return to labor for its services, it will come as near as you can come to it, probably.

Secretary Hurley—Would that be what is commonly termed in the world now as "Bolshevism"?

Mr. Marsh—If you want to designate an effort to achieve economic justice, which you say you want, as Bolshevism, you are entitled to so regard it. I should not regard it so; I should regard it as the best form of insurance for Americanism.

[86] *Ibid.*, pages 333–34.

Secretary Hurley—Let me ask this question: Would you want the Government to acquire title to everything in time of emergency?

Mr. Marsh—At least in time of war. Nothing else short of that is conscription of wealth, as far as I can see.

Secretary Hurley—Are you in favor of Government ownership in time of peace the same as in time of war?

Mr. Marsh—Of the things which, of themselves, in order to be efficiently operated, have got to be a monopoly; yes; not otherwise. If you mean I am a socialist; no.

Secretary Hurley—Then, of course, you are not a socialist?

Mr. Marsh—No.

Secretary Hurley—You are not a Bolshevist?

Mr. Marsh—That is quite obvious from my statements here.[87]

Tucker P. Smith, executive secretary of the Committee on Militarism in Education, was a bit vague and, at times, perilously in danger of sinking into a bog of abstractions.

. . . Wars in our day do not come out of the machinations and the deviltry of a few men in Washington, or of a few men in Wall Street; they come rather out of the long-time and broad national policies of imperialism and militarism and all of their ramifications, which bring nations to a point that may make it possible for small groups of individuals to be unusually influential. The thing the public should understand is this, that these particular policies to which they subscribe and which they in the main are in favor of carrying on in peace time, are the real causes of modern war, and that the mere catching of a few lucky profiteers will not make a fundamental difference in the making or in the frequency of war.[88]

[87] *Ibid.*, page 337.
[88] *Ibid.*, pages 678–79.

It would be quibbling to argue whether few or many men shape these "long-time and broad national policies of imperialism and militarism." The fact is that these policies are shaped to a considerable degree, by men who have axes to grind and who know just where and how to grind them. "The mere catching of a few lucky profiteers," obviously, may not "make a fundamental difference in the making or in the frequency of war." That is not basic. What is, as Mr. Smith himself writes, though in support of another thesis, is that the public does subscribe in peacetime to "particular policies."

Now, the age of miracles is over. "Particular policies" do not come from ectoplasm. They come from interested parties to whose profit it is to support their private opinions through the instrumentality of the press until they reappear under the guise of public opinion. To say, therefore, that

> the burdens of the World War are the burdens of war and not necessarily the burdens laid upon the people by a few groups of politicians and a few groups of capitalists. It is the war system itself which is bearing down upon humanity in this kind of world, and they may catch a few of those capitalists and they may catch a few of those politicians and make them goats, but war will go right on bearing down upon the rest of us, and the next one will bear much more heavily than the past. So we urge that your report point out that the only hope for really relieving the burdens of war upon man is to prevent war. That is the only way to make any material difference.—[89]

is as helpful as saying that the cause of disease is infection.

[89] *Ibid.*, page 679.

Mr. Smith was on firmer ground when he remarked that wars

result from a period, usually a long period, of all sorts of contentions and rivalries—the application of war methods to economic processes which bring us into a growing tension. Along with that goes our piling up of armaments in an effort to ward each other off, really increasing the tension; and, finally, the pile gets so high that it falls over.[90]

Mr. Hurley's questions brought the discussion around to military statistics, a field in which Mr. Smith is expert, and Mr. Hurley not so expert.

Secretary Hurley—Taking the size of the present Military Establishment of the United States, do you consider it of such magnitude as to be a menace to the peace or happiness of any other nation in the world?

Mr. Smith—I think, sir, the size of our Military Establishment has to be weighed over against our foreign policies, and I am sorry to say I think our constructive measures along lines of building peace machinery, and along lines of peace-minded economic policies, are not sufficiently great to compensate for what seems to be a smaller Military Establishment. Do you get my point of view?

Secretary Hurley—Yes, I do; but what I am trying to get at is you take the round figures, including some that are really not military components, but officers and men, constabulary, and so forth, amounting to 130,000 men out of 123,000,000 people, do you consider there is anything in that which appears overwhelming?

Mr. Smith—From our viewpoint, Mr. Chairman, the Military Establishment is much larger than 130,000 men. I think

[90] *Ibid.*, page 680.

the Military Establishment is all of those men who are in any way connected with our military affairs, and the number is much larger than 130,000, as you well know.

Secretary Hurley—Then you would include in the Military Establishment the National Guards of the States?

Mr. Smith—I would.

Secretary Hurley—And the citizens military training camps?

Mr. Smith—Yes.

Secretary Hurley—And the reserve officers' organization?

Mr. Smith.—From their political and psychological effects, most certainly, yes. Their military value is another question.

Secretary Hurley—Then you come down to the question of where our people, I believe, are traditionally opposed to a large standing army. Would you eliminate all training of civilians so as to save them hardships and possibly save their lives in time of emergency?

Mr. Smith—I am not sure I get specifically what you mean. Would you mind repeating?

Secretary Hurley—Well, you consider all these citizen components as part of the Military Establishment?

Mr. Smith—Yes, sir.[91]

For once at least Mr. Hurley's plugging of his theme song about the smallest standing army in the world on the basis of the country's population was silenced.

Norman Thomas, the present leader of American socialism, director of the League for Industrial Democracy and author of "America's Way Out," took the stand on May 20, 1931, after scuttling a gauche and brazen attempt by Mr. Hurley to exclude him and others of similar opinions from testifying at the hearings.

[91] *Ibid.*, pages 684–85.

At one o'clock on this day, the chairman announced that the Commission members had afternoon appointments.[92] Arthur A. Ballantine,[93] Assistant Secretary of the Treasury, had just concluded a tedious and lengthy history of war-time taxation. This announcement that the hearings were over for the day was made in spite of the fact that the executive secretary of the Commission had sent a telegram to Mr. Thomas who was then in North Dakota. The message stated:

> Extremely sorry that change of date inconveniences you stop it looks now as if no public hearings will be held after may twenty second stop program for twenty first and twenty second very full but if you cannot arrange otherwise we could find place for you on one of those two days stop very few witnesses are on the program for may twentieth and can give you plenty of time that day morning or afternoon if you can possibly make it stop

For a tense moment it seemed that Norman Thomas, at great inconvenience, had cancelled his lecture dates and come to Washington only to be informed by the Secretary of War that unfortunately the time was up, that the Secretary was sorry, etc., etc., and that he, the chairman of the Commission, was not responsible for the acts of the

[92] After Mr. Thomas' appearance before the Commission, however, Mr. Hurley risked the danger of Socialist contamination by inviting Mr. Thomas to lunch. . . . Mr. Thomas had another appointment.

[93] There is reason to believe that Mr. Ballantine was purposely brought in to testify on that day to give as little time as possible to Mr. Thomas. There is no proof at all, however, that Mr. Ballantine knew of this suspected maneuver.

executive secretary of the Commission, an official[94] who had arranged every appearance before the War Policies Commission. It was too raw. Even the press gagged at it. Mr. Hurley, after Mr. Thomas had firmly protested and asked just why he should be responsible for the acts of the executive secretary of the Commission, sensed the wind and cancelled his "appointments."

The Socialist leader endorsed Professor Lovett's proposal for a "planned national economy"[95] while pointing out that to socialize simply for war purposes would be to militarize the state in the eyes of the world, a policy which "would raise doubt against our good faith, whether justly or unjustly, since we were the chief sponsors of the Kellogg pact." He advocated a war against poverty which would diminish the general economic insecurity and the likelihood of war "by lessening the unscrupulous struggle for private profits in the world at large." He was

> thoroughly persuaded that the war against poverty in time of peace requires a planned economy and distribution for use, not profit, which inevitably must be based on social ownership of the principal means of production.

As aids for world disarmament Mr. Thomas proposed an international economic conference to wipe out the burden of war preparation and war taxes, recognition of Russia, the permanent withdrawal of marines "as missionaries to

[94] Robert H. Montgomery (Colonel of the Reserve Corps) was appointed executive secretary of the Commission at a salary of $750 a month. Why such a large salary was paid for this work has never been explained.

[95] *See* below, page 153 ff.

collect American debts," the joining of the World Court, and "probably of the League of Nations under restrictions which make sure we cannot go to war under article 10 or 16 to enforce peace." He was skeptical of war-time socialization of national wealth—Representative La Guardia had proposed to the Commission that the Government on the outbreak of a war "take over all industries and put all citizens on a ration basis"—on the ground that it might lead to fascism, was dubious of Mr. Baruch's price-fixing scheme, and was "certain that the cost-plus system is an abomination." He took a stand with Representative Ramseyer of Iowa, that one way of preventing war would be to pay for it as we go, adding that "from the standpoint of national economy, we can no more truly pay for the war after it is over in material goods than in men." He opposed the commissioning of industrialists in the Reserve Corps and the bestowal of war contracts on great corporations "for the purpose of sweetening the pill of war."

> These contracts consciously or unconsciously simply tend to militarize industry, and insidiously to harness the thinking of the manufacturers to the psychology and philosophy of a war machine.

Much to Mr. Thomas' annoyance Mr. Hurley asked him no questions.

Miss Dorothy Detzer, national executive secretary of the Women's International League for Peace and Freedom, argued that the promulgation of "war policies" is not only incongruous with promoting peace but also "contrary to the spirit and real meaning of the Kellogg-Briand treaty for the renunciation of war." Pointing out that the various interpretations of the Pact differentiating offensive from defensive war are only "a doctrinaire difference," she reminded the Commission that

> The important thing is the wording of the actual treaty. It is perfectly clear, perfectly simple, that every dispute shall be settled by pacific means, no matter what its origin. However, whatever the interpretation may be or however people may disagree on this point, the significance of the treaty lies, it seems to me, in the fact that the peoples of the world demanded that their governments should, through the most solemn and binding method known to governments, publicly declare the repudiation of the method of war for dealing with future disputes. In the treaty there is no suggestion that conflicts between nations will cease. In fact, the treaty assumes and anticipates future conflicts; but it definitely declares, as I have said before, that all of those disputes of whatever nature, or of whatever origin they may be, shall only be dealt with by pacific means.[96]

Her recommendation to eliminate peace-time profits in such war industries as munitions was perhaps the most important and practical one made to the Commission. "It would seem obvious," she said, "that if you would take the profits out of war you must first take the profits out of preparations for war; in other words, remove any private gain from preparation."

Miss Detzer, apparently, believes that a straight line is still the shortest distance between two points.

She was asked no questions.

[96] War Policies Commission Hearings, page 731.

John Nevin Sayre, executive secretary of the Fellowship of Reconciliation, also insisted on discussing the General Pact for the Renunciation of War. He warned the Commission that should it adopt General MacArthur's mobilization plan for drafting men between the ages of 18 and 45 the United States would be violating the spirit of the Kellogg-Briand Pact.

Mr. Sayre addressed the Congressional Caesars, leaving with them "resolutions on war and peace officially adopted in the last few years by some of the leading religious denominations[97] in this country" which he stated are "indicative of the sharpening conscience of the Christian Churches —a conscience which is bound to become more opposed to the war system during the coming decade, a conscience which this commission should not ignore, nor underestimate, nor violate." Nor will this "sharpening conscience," he warned the Commission, be wholly intangible.

> ... I am in a position to know that the movement of conscientious refusal to take part in war is making tremendous advances at this time. Recently a magazine of which I am president, the World To-morrow, sent out a questionnaire to 53,000 American ministers asking, among other questions:

[97] National Council of the Congregational Churches, Evangelical Synod, Methodist Episcopal General Conference, Methodist Episcopal Northeast Ohio Conference, Methodist Episcopal South General Conference, Lutheran Convention, Presbyterian General Assembly, Protestant Episcopal General Convention, Protestant Episcopal Lambeth Conference, General Synod of the Reformed Church in America, United Presbyterian Church General Assembly, Northern Baptist Convention, Southern Baptist Convention, International Convention of the Disciples of Christ, Reformed Presbyterian Synod.

> Are you personally prepared to state that it is your present purpose not to sanction any future war or participate as an armed combatant?
>
> Nineteen thousand three hundred and seventy-two ministers replied, and 10,427 answered with a straight "yes"; 12,076 said they believed "that the churches of America should now go on record as refusing to sanction or support any future war"; 16,018 said that they did not "favor military training in our public high schools and civilian colleges or universities." [98]

These sentiments, he added, "are held by a growing minority that counts," the significance of which "is not primarily in names or numbers but in its holding to and setting forth a principle of truth, a principle which corresponds to some of the deepest things in human nature, a principle which may be described in the words of Gandhi, of India, as 'truth force.' "

Addressing himself to a war axiom of Mr. Baruch which might very well have been written either by von Treitschke or Bernhardi,—

> Modern war requires that the full power of the Nation be exerted in the shortest possible time, not only to the violent beating down of the enemy by any destructive material force we can invent or use, but also to every process of slow and often insidious economic strangulation and political isolation that we can devise and administer.—

Mr. Sayre asked:

> Well, how can a Christian take part in that who expects to face the judgment of Christ and who hears in his conscience the voice of Christ saying:

[98] War Policies Commission Hearings, page 734.

Inasmuch as ye have done it unto one of the least of these, my brethren, ye have done it unto Me.

You are forcing him to choose between Christ and Caesar if Caesar insists that he must be one of the hundred and twenty-five million correlated moving parts all working to the violent beating down of human beings by any destructive material force that can be invented. The conscientious affirmer who refuses to do this is standing up for the liberty of the human soul against the tyranny of the war-making state.

In the second place, unless there is in the world a certain amount of thoroughgoing, uncompromising personal pacifism of the conscientious affirmer sort the peace movement will be doomed to failure. The war habit is not going to be put out of the way in this country or in any country easily. It is far too firmly intrenched. It can only be overcome by the spiritual power of men and women who will suffer and suffer and suffer for what they believe.[99]

There is every reason to believe that John Nevin Sayre fervently meant what he said and that he is prepared to suffer for his views. Regarding the Church, however, because of its deeds it is difficult to be convinced by its words against war. Its renunciation of war at a crucial time has yet to be tested. Unfortunately, the Church's failure before and during the World War to desist from assuring the masses in each country that the Divine Power was specially concerned with their interests is still vividly remembered.

Ten million dead, in addition to several millions hopelessly maimed bear eloquent testimony to this, the greatest betrayal in the history of man. The self-appointed disciples

[99] *Ibid.*, page 737.

of that being man calls God stand eternally convicted of perjury.

Institutions, like men, must be judged by their conduct in crises. We should lose not only a sense of direction, but what is equally important, a sense of comparative values, were this not true.

The problem of the Church and war may be discussed from another angle in what is perhaps a more concrete and lucid manner, that is, by considering what Mr. Sayre neglected to include in his passionate appeal to the Commission. It is the economic tie between the Church and the dominant industrial forces who—directly or indirectly—control the destiny of a nation. Many sincere, able and intelligent churchmen, it would seem, are unconscious of the fact that the Church, like the army, though only a pawn, nevertheless has an economic stake in war. Or if not in war, then in imperialistic policies which inevitably will lead and have led to war.

In other words, one must change the policies of the contributors to reshape the policies of the pulpit. It is this condition—the umbilical cord inexorably tying business to theology—which to a great degree is responsible for the difficulty the Church has in making itself felt. It is dubious, therefore, if even one-tenth of the 10,427 ministers whose "present purpose" it is "not to sanction any future war or participate as an armed combatant" will be able to afford a "truth force" in the face of the ruthless, pulverizing compulsion certain to be directed by the owners and employers of religion and opinion against those whose profession and mission it is to express their opinions. Under these conditions, as in the past, the terrific pressure of social ostracism and the crippling fear of poverty and starvation will be the weapons used to crumple the resolution of all but the strongest men. The "truth force" must make itself effective long before any danger of war exists if futile sacrifices are to be avoided.

Only when the philosophy of modern economic life changes will it be possible for a "truth force" to exert decisive influence. It has been said that political democracy will be attained through economic democracy and not economic through political democracy. Religious democracy will be attained in the same way.

The Proverbial Wolf—"Change What, Mr. Congressman?"

Dr. Arthur Deerin Call, the secretary of the American Peace Society, saw the Commission faced with no problems other than those pertaining to war. Following this theme he delivered perhaps the best war preparedness speech of all the witnesses, including the several generals, who appeared before the Commission. He said:

> It has been commonly recognized, certainly since the time of Cicero, that in time of war laws are silent. When people go to war, they must be prepared to place all their laws aside and to fare forth to kill and to destroy to the uttermost, if need be, quite lawlessly. That is the grim ugliness at the heart of war.[100]

And later on:

[100] *Ibid.*, page 756.

My feeling is that if we are faced with war, the only thing to do is to fare forth and win it.[101]

On as late a date as nearly two months prior to Dr. Call's appearance before the War Policies Commission, counsel for the Bethlehem Steel Corporation testified, in a suit brought by the Government for $11,000,000 alleged excess profits, that "the United States Steel Corporation made a profit on wartime contracts of more than 50 per cent, as compared with the Bethlehem Shipbuilding Corporation's profits of 21 per cent." The Associated Press story as published in the New York Times of April 5, 1931, stated:

WAR PROFIT ON STEEL PUT AT 50 PER CENT.

Bethlehem Counsel Testifies That Is What the Steel Corporation Received.

Philadelphia, April 4 (AP).—Testimony was given today that the United States Steel Corporation made a profit on wartime contracts of more than 50 per cent, as compared with the Bethlehem Shipbuilding Corporation's profits of 21 per cent.

Ralph B. Evans, chief counsel for Bethlehem, so testified in the suit brought against the Bethlehem Steel Corporation and subsidiaries by the government for $11,000,000 alleged excess profits. . . .

Yet, in spite of this testimony and the mass of undisputed statistics on the outrageous war profiteering, not only in steel but in nearly every other basic commodity, Dr. Call calmly declared, "We very much doubt the necessity for additional legislation to eliminate unjust profiteer-

[101] *Ibid.*, page 757.

ing."[102] Just profiteering, it seems, is acceptable to the man who was introduced to the Commission as the secretary of the American Peace Society and editor of the Advocate of Peace, the executive secretary of the American Group of the Interparliamentary Union, the delegate to National Peace Congresses and president of the Connecticut Peace Society from 1906 to 1912, the director of the International Peace Bureau at Berne and director of the twenty-third conference of the Interparliamentary Union and the recipient of the Chevalier of the Legion of Honor of France. It would be interesting to hear his views on moral murder.

Showing the same concern for protecting wealth and property in war-time from the rigors of conscription as he did for minimizing the significance of the huge war profits made by industrialists and financiers, Dr. Call categorically opposed the conscription of wealth and property by the Government in war-time.

> Another question facing the War Policies Commission is, "Shall private property be taken for public use during war?" The answer to this question is that it was taken during the late war and may be taken during the next war. The only qualification is that there must be just compensation. The inquiry, therefore, boils down to this: Should the Government be given the power to conscript private property without just compensation? Our reply to this question is "No."[103]

Dr. Call evidently does not share the War Department's confidence in our "patriotic industrialists."

[102] *Ibid.*, page 754.
[103] *Ibid.*, page 755.

Since efficiency is the measure of success in war, and since efficiency without profits is sure to break down, at least in certain lines, it is well to keep the possibilities of profit alive; not exorbitant profits, but some profits. For the same utilitarian purpose, at least, the institution and rights of private property should be maintained in time of war. Every selfish motive will and should be utilized when once war has broken upon a people. All subordination of private interests in time of war should be as painless as possible.[104]

After this paean to war-time profits he solved the problem of war in the abstract by telling the Commission that all of its objectives, "these highly desired ends," could be accomplished "by avoiding war." Lip service to "avoiding war," a sentiment subscribed to by every militarist and ammunition manufacturer, with a good word for every camp, followed:

It is generally accepted by our people that we must have an Army and a Navy. Since we must have an Army and a Navy, it is plain good judgment that the Army and Navy should be the best, not the largest, Army; and the best, not the biggest, Navy, that our military experts can provide. In the language of George Washington, we shall have to take care "always to keep ourselves, by suitable establishments, on a respectable defensive posture." But, to quote again from the Father of Our Country, we needs must: "Observe good faith and justice toward all nations; cultivate peace and harmony with all." And, to quote again from that immortal Farewell Address, it is of prime importance that we "avoid the necessity of those overgrown military establishments which, under any form of government, are inauspicious to liberty

[104] *Ibid.*, page 756.

and which are to be regarded as particularly hostile to republican liberty." [105]

And after this pious straddling, Representative Hadley placed the mantle of respectability on Dr. Call's shoulders —a gesture intended to separate him from such "radical" people as Dorothy Detzer, John Nevin Sayre, Tucker P. Smith and Norman Thomas.

Mr. Hadley—Doctor, just one question: You had a very thoughtful analysis of what has gone before here, before concluding with your general observation on peace. Quoting part of the title, which you did, is it your thought that reasonable preparation for war, in the event of war, tends to promote peace, or to subvent it?

Doctor Call—I have been 20 years studying that question, and I can not answer it. I have only general ideas on the subject. I am quite of the opinion that the "reasonable defensive posture," as phrased by President Washington, remains still a necessary posture on the part of our people. So long as our Army is as small as it is, I can not see how any major power in the world can look upon us as in any sense a danger. It is true, I believe, that we could not wage a war in a foreign country by our Navy alone; it has to be waged by the Navy in cooperation with the Army. Since our Army is as small as it is, I am of the opinion that our Military Establishment as is does not constitute, therefore, a menace to the peace of the world and that it is not necessary to think that it does.

Mr. Hadley—I asked you that question because of some of those who have spoken, having the same end in view you have—the ultimate desideratum of peace—have taken a contrary view to that which you have just expressed.[106]

[105] *Ibid.*, page 756.

[106] *Ibid.*, pages 756–57.

Representative Collins supplied the only discordant note to the love feast.

Mr. Collins—Doctor, you seem to be strong for the status quo: is that it?

Doctor Call—I would not ignore the status quo.

Mr. Collins—Well, are you not for the status quo?

Doctor Call—No, sir.

Mr. Collins—You are not?

Doctor Call—No, sir.

Mr. Collins—Does not your statement indicate it?

Doctor Call—We are living in a living world.

Mr. Collins—Yes; and everything you advocate is the doctrine of a hundred years ago?

Doctor Call—Well, I do not know of any better doctrine than the doctrine that was established in 1787.

Mr. Collins—In the event we have another war, you think it ought to be conducted as the late one? I take that from your statement?

Doctor Call—I sincerely hope that we shall not have another war.

Mr. Collins—I understand that. There is not a man in the Army or Navy but will say that.

Doctor Call—I think so.

Mr. Collins—But in the event of a war, you are for its conduct the same as the late war was conducted?

Doctor Call—I could answer that question by yes or no; but I doubt if a yes or no answer would exactly answer the question. My feeling is that if we are faced with war, the only thing to do is to fare forth and win it.

Mr. Collins—And to conduct it as the late war was conducted?

Doctor Call—Oh, I can not say that; no, sir.

Mr. Collins—Well, everything that you set out in your statement is in line with the way the late one was conducted. You have not suggested anything new; the things you suggested are the identical things that we did in the late war. You even defended the profiteers. Do you know the size of our Army?

Dr. Call—I do not defend war profiteers, sir. As for the Army, I understand it is between one hundred and two hundred thousand.

Mr. Collins—I thought that. We have 136,000 men in our Army; we have 190,000 men in the National Guards; we have about 110,000 to 115,000 men in the Reserve Officers Training Corps, a little more than that in the Organized Reserves; we train about 40,000 in the citizens military training and, including the persons in civilian life who perform a larger service than the enlisted men in the Army, we have around 800,000 men.

Doctor Call—They are not all in the Army, are they, Congressman?

Mr. Collins—Oh, they are subject to be taken into the Army immediately. In the National Guard enlisted personnel we have a better class of soldier than in the enlisted personnel of the Regular Army. Now there is not any use in hiding anything in this situation. We want to tell the truth about it, and the idea of letting the world think we have an army of 100,000 or 125,000 is just hiding the truth. And its cost, I dare say, is larger than the cost of any other military establishment in the world.

That is all I have to say.[107]

Shortly after agreeing with Secretary Hurley's statement—couched in a form known to the legal profession as leading—namely, that he, Dr. Call, wasn't for the status quo but "as a matter of fact . . . referred to the national de-

107 *Ibid.*, pages 757–58.

fense act of 1920, which was the method of Congress for correcting the unwise economic principles followed at times during the late war," he admitted to Mr. Collins that not only had he not suggested anything to the Commission as far as equalizing the burdens of war but also that he didn't "know enough to approve or disapprove" of the national defense act of 1920.

Secretary Hurley—In response to a question by Congressman Collins you seemed to intimate your remarks were directed to conducting the economics of the next war as the last was conducted. As a matter of fact, you referred to the national defense act of 1920, which was the method of Congress for correcting the unwise economic principles followed at times during the late war. Did you not take that as the basis of your statement?

Doctor Call—Quite so.

Secretary Hurley—You would not like what you have said to indicate you wanted no improvement over the late war, or no greater attempt to equalize the burdens of war?

Doctor Call—Quite the contrary.

Secretary Hurley—Your purpose is to equalize, as far as that be possible, and to eliminate all profits of war?

Doctor Call—That is my position.

Secretary Hurley—You, of course, conclude that the only way to do this is to avoid war?

Doctor Call—Yes, sir.

Secretary Hurley—But you do not contend this commission should not go as far as it may with the enlightenment it receives to attempt to equalize, or possibly I should say further, to remove, the inequalities of the burdens of war, and to eliminate profiteering?

Doctor Call—I wish you Godspeed, but I fear that you will not get very far in that particular.

Secretary Hurley—You have referred to the fact this is a living world. In a living world economic, political, and social conditions constantly change, do they not?

Doctor Call—That is the way I understand it.

Secretary Hurley—Do you object to those charged with the responsibility of defense of the Nation attempting to change the conditions of preparation for defense with the changing social, political, and economic conditions?

Doctor Call—Manifestly, that will have to be done.

Mr. Collins—Well, what have you suggested to change them?

Doctor Call—Change what, Mr. Congressman?

Mr. Collins—The conditions, so as more nearly to equalize the burdens of war. You have not suggested anything to this commission.

Doctor Call—I am inclined to agree with you, and I am sorry.

Mr. Collins—Do you approve the national defense act?

Doctor Call—I do not know enough to approve or disapprove.

Mr. Collins—That is all.[108]

In an "additional statement," presumably mailed to the Commission some time after his appearance on the stand, Dr. Call rivals Voltaire's inimitable Dr. Pangloss in his optimistic expectations on what will come from the War Policies Commission's deliberations. He wrote:

A peace policies commission in this country, supplemented as far as possible by similar commissions in other countries studying these questions such as we have here proposed, would be a normal outcome of the War Policies Commission. Such

[108] *Ibid.*, page 759.

a work might show nations how to soften violence and exaggeration with common sense and to substitute the ways of reason and persuasion for the follies of force. If this be the outcome, the War Policies Commission may find that it has aided the peace movement more effectively than as yet it seems to suspect.[109]

Perhaps Dr. Call, who made not one reference to the General Pact for the Renunciation[110] of War, did aim—in the words of Representative Hadley—at the ultimate desideratum of peace. Unfortunately, however, his approach to the problem, though supported by quotations from George Washington, is so vague and so "ultimate" that it fails to offer tangible hope to those who desire to break the vicious circle of competing armaments.

[109] *Ibid.*, page 854.

[110] Known more popularly as the Pact of Paris, the Kellogg Pact or Kellogg Treaty, and the Kellogg-Briand Pact.

CHAPTER SIX

OFFICIALLY "MINIMIZING" WAR PROFITS

On March 5, 1932, one year after its first public session and after hearing nearly fifty witnesses and taking over eight hundred pages of testimony the War Policies Commission sent in its final reports to the President. The latter turned it over to Congress two days later.

In the main, the twelve to one majority final report recommended: (1) that a constitutional amendment be adopted to eliminate all doubt about the power of Congress "to prevent profiteering and to stabilize prices in time of war;" (2) that in the meantime the revenue law should provide for the recapture of excess profits by taxing 95 per cent of all individual and corporation income above the average profit made by the individual or corporation during the three years immediately preceding a war; (3) that Congress should consider no constitutional amendment to permit the taking of private property for public use in wartime without compensation.[111]

The majority and minority final reports, which together filled one newspaper column, follow:

[111] The resolution of Senators Vandenberg of Michigan, Reed of Pennsylvania, Robinson of Indiana and Swanson of Virginia asking Secretary of the Treasury Mills to advise the Senate on the best method of applying the proposed 95 per cent tax was adopted.

Report of Commission Created by Public Resolution No. 98, Seventy-First Congress, Approved June 27, 1930

March 5, 1932.

To the President:

The commission appointed under Public Resolution No. 98, Seventy-first Congress, entitled "Joint resolution to promote peace and to equalize the burdens and to minimize the profits of war," respectfully submits the following report and recommendations:

First. We recommend, in order to eliminate all doubt concerning the extent of the power of the Congress to prevent profiteering and to stabilize prices in time of war, that a proposed constitutional amendment clearly defining such power be submitted by the Congress to the States.

Second. We further recommend that until a constitutional amendment be adopted clearly defining the power of Congress to prevent profiteering and to stabilize prices in time of war, the following program be adopted as governmental policy in order effectively to minimize the profits of war and to distribute its burdens and sacrifices equitably:

(a) That the Congress should empower the President, in the event of war, to institute a program under which prices may be stabilized and thereafter adjusted at such levels as will minimize inflation and will secure to the Government the use of any private property needed in the prosecution of the war without affording the owner thereof profit due to the war. It should be clearly stated that such a program will not be placed in operation until Congress specifically directs it as a necessary measure in the conduct of the war.

(b) The Congress should empower the President to make, in war, such readjustments in, and additions to, the executive departments of the Government as are necessary to assure adequate control of all national resources. The President should be empowered also to fix the status, for the period of the war, of personnel transferred under this authority, from one bureau or department of the Government to any other.

(c) Existing law empowering the President to compel acceptance of war orders and to commandeer property should be continued.

(d) In addition to all other plans to remove the profits of war, the revenue law should provide that, upon any declaration of war and during the period of such emergency, individuals and corporations shall be taxed 95 per cent of all income above the previous three-year average, with proper adjustments for capital expenditures for war purposes by existing or new industries.

(e) In time of peace continuous planning by the Federal Government, particularly by the War and Navy Departments, should be directed toward insuring:

(1) That upon declaration of war there shall be immediately available to the Congress accurate and detailed estimates concerning the man-power and material needs of the military and naval services, together with detailed studies and recommendations concerning the most applicable methods for mobilizing the necessary men and procuring the required munitions.

(2) That there shall be no competitive bidding between Government agencies for the products of industry.

(3) There shall be no placing of contracts in excess of needs.

(4) That cost plus percentage methods of purchase shall be eliminated.

(5) That the munitions production load shall be distributed properly over the United States.

(6) That the governmental organizations required in the administration of war functions shall be set up promptly.

(7) That the necessary controls respecting prices, raw ma-

terials, transportation, priorities, war trade, finances, and related matters shall be continuously studied, so that in the event of war the will of Congress may be promptly and efficiently administered.

(f) Plans prepared in the War and Navy Departments for the accomplishment of the above should be continuously revised to meet changing national and international conditions, and should be thoroughly examined and revised at least every two years by appropriate congressional committees.

Third. We recommend that no constitutional amendment to permit the taking of private property in time of war without compensation be considered by the Congress.

Respectfully submitted.

Patrick J. Hurley,
Chairman

David A. Reed,
Vice Chairman

Joe T. Robinson
John J. McSwain
Arthur H. Vandenberg
William D. Mitchell
C. F. Adams
R. P. Lamont
Wm. P. Holaday
Arthur M. Hyde
W. N. Doak

Lindley H. Hadley,
Secretary.

Absent: Senator Claude A. Swanson, attending the conference at Geneva.

MINORITY REPORT

Congress of the United States,
House of Representatives,
Committee on Appropriations,
Washington, D.C., March 3, 1932.

To the President:

The purpose in creating the so-called War Policies Commission was to "study and consider amending the Constitution of the United States to provide that private property may be taken by Congress for public use during war and methods of equalizing the burdens and to remove the profits of war, together with a study of policies to be pursued in the event of war."

I take it that the object of the resolution creating the commission deals solely with the purpose of eliminating profits that accrue to certain classes of individuals and corporations during war and that "a study of policies to be pursued in the event of war" relates to policies to be prescribed by Congress either through a constitutional amendment or by legislation for the purpose of eliminating war profits.

As the Constitution of the United States is now drawn I am convinced that the only way to eliminate war profits is through the adoption of a constitutional amendment so as to enable Congress to pass legislation creating an agency to fix prices of commodities, either for the purpose of keeping profits at a minimum or the entire elimination of them. I heartily favor the adoption of a constitutional amendment to carry out this object.

I do not believe it was the intention of Congress that the power to fix prices of commodities should be delegated to military men. I believe that such administrative matters should be entirely in the hands of civilians, and I object to any recommendation that would tend to confer upon military men the power to regulate prices or the activities of the civilian population during war or at any other time. I am firmly convinced, whether intended or not, that any war planning as now carried on by the War Department will in the end result in the administration of price fixing laws and the regulation of civilian activities by military and naval officers if the recommendations of the majority members of the commission are finally adopted by Congress.

I regret that I am unable to follow the majority of the members of the commission upon all of their proposals and respectfully submit to you this dissent.

Very respectfully,
Ross A. Collins.[112]

Libretto

It was clear from the outset of the hearings that nothing would be recommended which would even whisper substantial modification of the holy Fifth Amendment, that is, suggest anything that would interfere with profits to business in war-time. The provisions of the Commission's final report were surprising only in that they proved early expectations too conservative.

It was the finale of a tragic comic opera which was played under the heading: minimizing the profits of war with an obligato scored for lip service to distributing war's "burdens and sacrifices equitably." Its definition of the profits of war is identical with that stressed by the indus-

[112] *Congressional Record,* March 7, 1932, pages 5524–25.

trialists who appeared before it on the stand—simply those returns above the so-called normal or peace-time rate.

The Commission's recommended program, adopted ostensibly "to minimize the profits of war and to distribute its burdens and sacrifices equitably" is nothing more nor less than a scheme to insure normal peace-time profits or the familiar fair return on the investment to business in war-time. Lest there be any doubt on that score the Commission recommended "that no constitutional amendment to permit the taking of private property in time of war without compensation be considered by the Congress." By compensation it could only mean "just compensation." And "just compensation," as we saw in the Baltimore Street Railway Case, meant a return of more than 7.44 per cent on the investment.[113]

In its final report the Commission violated clear instructions given it by Congress. Criticism of the Commission's failure to carry out its instructions and the basic injustice of its final report was made in a trenchant editorial which appeared on March 14, 1932, in the Washington, D. C., Daily *News,* and later, in other Scripps-Howard newspapers.

War Profits

Last year's hope that modern statesmanship might turn to the most promising of all peace proposals—the elimination of profit from war—has perished with the final report of the Federal War Policies Commission.

113 *See* above, note 17.

Twelve of the fourteen men directed last year to draw plans for amending the Constitution so that private property might be drafted when war descends upon us just as men are drafted, have come to the conclusion that this should not even be considered by Congress. Instead they suggest that the President be empowered in war-time to "stabilize" prices at a level which will minimize inflation. Only one member of the commission was able to remember with sympathy the original task to which the commission was assigned.

Of course, with the utmost sincerity and idealism it would be impossible for a government to equalize the burden of war between a man whose life is taken from him, and a man who merely loses his property. It would make little difference to a man lying mortally wounded on some future battlefield to know that the folks safe at home were doing without the regulated profits which the War Policies Commission thinks they should be allowed.

But it was the hope of the men who conceived the plan, for elimination of profits and for confiscation of needed property, that war might occur much less frequently if it were known in advance by munition makers and their bankers and all the thousands of business men who might be affected that war would mean acute financial suffering for them, instead of profiteering.

Fortunately there is little prospect that the *inadequate, unsatisfactory recommendations* of the War Policies Commission majority will be acted upon at this session of Congress. (Author's italics.)

After insulating war-time profits, the Commission impotently gestured towards recapturing excess profits.

(d) In addition to all other plans to remove the profits of war, the revenue law should provide that, upon any declaration of war and during the period of such emergency, individuals and corporations shall be taxed 95 per cent of all income above the previous three-year average, with proper adjustments for capital expenditures for war purposes by existing or new industries.[114]

The Commission's prescription for distributing war-time "burdens and sacrifices equitably" is indeed a generous one. It failed, however, to specify just how a concern which has made, for instance, an average of 10 per cent in the previous three years will make any war-time sacrifice even remotely proportionate to that made by the poor devil who must face physical incapacitation or death, if it is to receive the same 10 per cent in war-time.

Secondly, those corporations which have made, let us say, only a 3 per cent profit during this three-year period need have little fear of this provision in the light of the joker contained in the qualification which allows corporations "proper adjustments for capital expenditures for war purposes by existing or new industries." These "proper adjustments" may be expected to breed incalculable corrupt practices if corporation accountants are as ingenious as they were in the last war. Ingenuity may not even be necessary in view of the fact that the heads of each industry will indubitably preside over the various military-business price-fixing boards inevitable in war-time which will dictate prices in their own fields.

Thirdly, this provision fails to treat the certainty of huge profits through bulk war orders even if the concern in

114 *Congressional Record,* March 7, 1932, page 5525.

question had made only a 3 per cent return during the years previous to a declaration of war. In other words, this provision neglects to provide against the absolute amounts of profit returns.

From the standpoint of the principle back of the resolution such a war-time guarantee to business has little to do with equalizing the human and economic burdens of war. It pays even less attention to the mountain of official data, especially war records, proving the impossibility of preventing business fraud and the impracticability of accurately supervising corporation accounts.

Thus the Commission emphasized the notorious disparity between titles to Congressional resolutions, the resolutions themselves and reports made on them. Although acting under a resolution entitled a "joint resolution to promote peace and to equalize the burdens and to minimize the profits of war," the Commission made a report which had as much to do with equalizing the burdens of war and promoting peace as the "to protect American labor" phrase in the title of the Hawley-Smoot tariff act has to do with the welfare of the American laborer. It is not necessary to elaborate on the unbridgeable gap between a resolution directing the adoption of legislation to eliminate profit in war-time and a program to fix "normal" profits in war-time. It is sufficient to point out that there is absolutely no mention in the body of the resolution creating the War Policies Commission about "minimizing" the profits in war-time. Rather, it specifically directed the members to consider amending the Constitution, not to minimize but to eliminate profits in war-time and to equalize the burdens thereof.

Other recommendations in the report are directly concerned with such war policies as estimates on man power and material needs of the military and naval services, munitions, the prompt setting up of "governmental organizations" for the "administration of war functions" and the continuous study of "the necessary controls respecting prices, raw materials, transportation, priorities, war trade, finances, and related matters" so that "in the event of war the will of Congress may be promptly and efficiently administered." To accomplish all this the Commission recommended that the war plans being prepared in the War and Navy Departments should be "continuously revised to meet changing national and international conditions, and should be thoroughly examined and revised at least every two years by appropriate congressional committees." If all this means a provocative "war policies" commission every two years, it is to be deprecated as a dangerously irritating war-provoking national policy.[115]

A minute examination of the final report fails to disclose any reference to that part of the title concerning the intention "to promote peace." It seems that perhaps the Commission's energies were exhausted by the preparation of its profits-fixing program under a resolution directing it to eliminate war-time profits so that capital and property could be drafted as a man is drafted.

[115] Ostensibly under the National Defense Act.

The "Minority" Report

The minority or final report of Representative Collins was anti-climatic and disappointing—even to those inured to the reality of political expediency—in the light of his withering cross-examination throughout the hearings of both jingoes and representatives of big business.

At one of the November secret meetings of the Commission Mr. Collins[116] had read a three-point proposal to the

[116] In November, 1931, the members of the Commission were presented by the War Department with a printed fifty-four page "Tentative Draft for Consideration by Members of the Commission Created by Public Resolution No. 98, 71st Congress" which was written with a view to having it adopted as the Commission's final report. This secret document, which was rejected by the Commission by a slender vote, stated categorically that no constitutional amendment was necessary to fix prices in war-time on both constitutional and general grounds. This Report, in spite of the obvious viciousness of General MacArthur's proposal for a guaranteed 6 per cent profit based on "what it is claimed is the investment" asked the Commission to officially adopt the War Department Mobilization Plan hook, line and sinker, by adopting as its own the following statement: "The commission desires to commend the comprehensive War Department plan. It is well conceived and bears the mark of understanding and skillful executives. The commission does not feel competent to criticize the details of its military procurement plans and policies and suggests that unless and until constructive criticisms and suggestions are offered the assumption is justified that the United States has as good a plan as can be devised."

Mr. Collins, after taking issue with this statement, read the following recommendations to the Commission:

RECOMMENDATIONS

In compliance with Public Resolution No. 98, Congressman Ross Collins submits for adoption by the Commission the following:

(1) The establishment of a National Economic Council.

The Commission recommends (a) that an advisory economic council shall be established. Its functions shall be to study economic and social

Commission. He advocated then a constitutional amendment which would permit Congress to take private property in war-time "without compensation therefor." He also recommended the establishment of an advisory economic council which should "cooperate with existing agencies in working out economic policies which may serve to promote peaceful trade relations with other nations. The National Economic Council shall advise with the economic councils of other nations for the purpose of studying ways and

conditions of the United States and to formulate policies which will tend to promote cooperation among all the participants in agriculture, industry and business, and a more just and equitable participation in, and sharing of the fruits of, the nation's wealth, industry and economic opportunities, by all of the people of the United States. (b) This Council shall also cooperate with existing agencies in working out economic policies which may serve to promote peaceful trade relations with other nations. (c) The National Economic Council shall advise with the economic councils of other nations for the purpose of studyings ways and means of carrying on trade and otherwise maintaining international trade relations in the interest of continued peace between nations.

(2) The recommendation to Congress of the passing of a Joint Resolution proposing an amendment to the Constitution of the United States, which reads:

"ARTICLE ——"

"During a war in which the United States is engaged, Congress shall have the power to take private property without compensation therefor."

(3) The recommendation to Congress of the passing of a Joint Resolution proposing an amendment to the Constitution of the United States, which reads:

"ARTICLE ——"

"The making or renewal of any loan to the Government or national of any nation engaged in armed conflict is prohibited, unless the United States is engaged in such conflict as an ally of such nation.

"Congress shall have the power to enforce this article by appropriate legislation."

means of carrying on trade and otherwise maintaining international trade relations in the interest of continued peace between nations."

His third recommendation proposed a second amendment to the Constitution which would prohibit "the making or renewal of any loan to the Government or national of any nation engaged in armed conflict . . . unless the United States is engaged in such conflict as an ally of such nation."

At the showdown, however, Mr. Collins was "convinced that the only way to eliminate war profits is through the adoption of a constitutional amendment so as to enable Congress to pass legislation creating an agency to fix prices of commodities, *either for the purpose of keeping profits at a minimum or the entire elimination of them.*" (Author's italics.) The provision for "keeping profits at a minimum," in addition to emasculating the suggestion for the "entire elimination" of war-time profits, makes it difficult to understand just what is the substantial difference between the majority and minority reports.

But, fortunately for the public, the change on the part of Mr. Collins, which may have been dictated by either temperament or political expediency, will not destroy the importance to the public interest of his cross-examination during the hearings.

However, in justice to Mr. Collins, it must be said that he did not wholly desert his original standard. On March 9th, two days after the presentation of the majority report by Senator Vandenberg to the Senate, he inserted in the

Congressional Record the identical recommendations he had submitted in November for adoption by the Commission. Just why he did not see fit to give these recommendations the importance of incorporation in his final report he has never satisfactorily explained to the considerable following who expected him to stand up to his convictions—that is, his November convictions. In other words, if he really believed in the recommendations he considered important enough to submit to the Commission in November why he did drop them from his final report in March? And if further study had purged him of his November convictions, why did he insert them in the Congressional Record?

A Mouse on the Senate Floor

Senator Vandenberg of Michigan, a member of the Commission, introduced and defended the final report on the floor of the Senate on March 7, 1932.[117]

"Let none misunderstand the final purpose we have sought to serve in this whole connection," he said. "It is not to facilitate war. It is to discourage it if a commercial motive should ever influence such decisions, and to democratize it if, despite all honorable efforts, it comes."

Speaking for the twelve members who signed the final report, he dismissed the idea of "drafting capital" in wartime as an "abstractly laudable notion," but unfortunately "an impractical impossibility" (sic!). Nevertheless, he said,

[117] No debate was held that day on the report in the House of Representatives.

"the commission is practically unanimous in the view that it has achieved a formula which better reaches the objective and which accomplishes everything the original order of Congress had in its purview and which *totally answers the aspirations of the American Legion* as expressed for the last decade and repeatedly stressed in its annual conventions and as shared by all straight thinkers with a proper conception of the relative duties and obligations incumbent upon all citizens in a democracy." (Author's italics.)

Senator Clarence C. Dill of Washington, one of those who in his own words, "had considerable to do with the passage of the joint resolution" was amazed at the Commission report. Perplexed, he asked:

> Mr. President, this is the recommendation of the commission, so far as the Senate is concerned, to carry out the proposal of the American Legion that we shall draft property the same as we draft men?

And a minute later:

> And when we are proposing to amend the Constitution it is suggested by the commission to amend it only so that the Government can fix profits, not prevent profits?

Senator Borah, evidently addressing himself to that part of the title "joint resolution to promote peace," inferred that if profits on munitions, for example, cannot be prevented in peace-time they certainly cannot be eliminated in the hurly-burly of war-time. He asked:

> And the question of doing the same thing in time of peace did not come before the committee?

Mr. Vandenberg—It did not. It could not. It is not a part of our problem. It is unrelated because the régimes of peace and war inevitably involve totally different conceptions and necessities. All of us consent to rules in time of war which would be unthinkable in times of peace.

In short, though the cries of the wounded and maimed of the last great slaughter are still to be heard, plans are already being made to arrange for profits in the next war.

Mr. Dill—And the commission has recommended an amendment, not to take the profit out of war but to give the Congress the right to limit the profit, to fix the profit.

Mr. Vandenberg—On the contrary——

Mr. Dill—In other words, it looks to me as though the commission in this situation is like the mountain that labored and brought forth a mouse.

Senator Dill evidently did not agree with Senator Vandenberg that the final report "accomplishes everything the original order of Congress had in its purview and which totally answers the aspirations of the American Legion as expressed for the last decade and repeatedly stressed in its annual conventions and as shared by all straight thinkers with a proper conception of the relative duties and obligations incumbent upon all citizens in a democracy."

Mr. Dill—Mr. President, before the Senator takes his seat, I want to know what reason the committee had for refusing to recommend a constitutional amendment that would carry out the great plan which the American Legion so enthusiastically put forward looking to the enactment of laws that would enable Congress to draft property in time of war the same as it drafts men.

Mr. Vandenberg—To answer the Senator's question with any finality would require me to enter upon a discussion which would be longer, I am sure, than the Senator would desire to precipitate at the moment. Let me answer him just to this extent: In seeking to equalize—let me emphasize the verb "equalize"—the burdens of war it was speedily disclosed by the witnesses before the commission that an arbitrary drafting of property might actually create a larger discrepancy in the burden of war through the drafting of one unit in a given industry and the release of the other units from any such imposition.

Mr. Dill—Mr. President——

Mr. Vandenberg—Let me finish. The commission came to the conclusion, based, I believe and as I recall, upon the preponderating weight of the testimony,[118] that the ultimate recapture of any profits accruing from the operation of war adequately and in practical fashion accomplished all that the Senator has in mind.

But the Senator from Washington was persistent:

Mr. Dill—Let me ask the Senator where does he get the principle of which he speaks, namely, the equalizing of profits to individuals and to property. There was nothing to that effect in the resolution that was adopted appointing the commission of which the Senator is a member. That resolution looked to the taking out of war the profits on property used in war; and yet the commission comes back here and recommends that we go to the great trouble of amending the Constitution of the United States, without including within the power given Congress the right of Congress to exercise its

[118] The Michigan Senator failed to state that the overwhelming number of witnesses were industrialists and military men who stand to gain by war, some of whom were directly connected with the United States military-industrial management of the last war.

judgment on that question, if ever the time should come when it wanted to take that step. I want to know where the Senator gets the equalization idea of which he speaks.

Mr. Vandenberg—I remind the Senator that the instructions to the commission included the admonition to undertake an equalization of the burdens as well as the prohibition of war profits.

Mr. Dill—But we have a right now to limit the profits.

Mr. Vandenberg—The Senator's present argument, going to the merits of the case, may very appropriately be addressed to the Judiciary Committee. I am simply submitting the findings of the commission after one year's intimate study in contact with the best authority and advice that we could procure.

Mr. Dill—I am a member of the Judiciary Committee, but the point I am trying to make is this: I had considerable to do with the passage of the joint resolution. The joint resolution specifically was directed to taking the profit out of war.

Mr. Vandenberg—And we think we have done that.

And then Senator Dill gave his vivid description of the Commission's final report to the country.

Mr. Dill—And the commission has recommended an amendment, not to take the profit out of war but to give the Congress the right to limit the profit, to fix the profit.

Mr. Vandenberg—On the contrary——

Mr. Dill—In other words, it looks to me as though the commission in this situation is like the mountain that labored and brought forth a mouse.

Mr. Vandenberg—That may be the Senator's view. I think it is not the view of the Senator from Arkansas [Mr. Robinson] or the Senator from Pennsylvania [Mr. Reed] or the Members of the House or the members of the Cabinet who labored for one year upon this problem. If the specific and tangible removal of 95 per cent of the profits of war is not a direct frontal attack upon war profiteering, then I do not know how to make it.

Indeed, the Commission has brought forth a mouse—one which can scarcely be expected to gnaw at the profit sacks.

CHAPTER SEVEN

BASIC PROBLEMS AND METHODS

Clearly, the very phrase "war policies" is incongruous with the words of the General Pact for the Renunciation of War the entire body of which is constitutionally a part of the law of the United States. The Pact, which by February 13, 1932, had been signed by fifty-nine nations, reads:

Article I

The High Contracting Parties solemnly declare in the names of their respective peoples that they condemn recourse to war for the solution of international controversies, and renounce it as an instrument of national policy in their relations with one another.

Article II

The High Contracting Parties agree that the settlement or solution of all disputes or conflicts of whatever nature or of whatever origin they may be, which may arise among them, shall never be sought except by pacific means.

In spite of the lucid language of the Pact, especially that of Article II, thus far most statesmen have insisted upon reading into it a defensive interpretation to the effect that the Pact does not disallow a war of defense.

This view is countered by the argument that if such a differentiation is tenable we are practically just where we started, inasmuch as no power will ever admit that it is declaring an aggressive war. It is argued that the signatories of the Pact not only have condemned war but have renounced it "as an instrument of national policy." Article II specifically states that the powers will not settle any "dispute or conflict of whatever nature or of whatever origin . . . except by pacific means." Now, no war begins without a dispute or the existence of a conflict, real or assumed. Therefore, since we have solemnly agreed to settle these disputes or conflicts, heretofore the inevitable precursor of war, by "pacific means," the declaration of war or participation in what amounts to a state of war constitutes a violation of the Pact. Furthermore, the argument continues, inherent in the problem is a conflict between the United States Constitution and the Pact or Treaty since an act of Congress may repeal a treaty. To overcome this obstacle it is suggested that the Constitution should be amended so that Congress will not have power to declare war, thereby removing a potential destroyer of the Pact.

This interpretation was strengthened by a resolution introduced on February 5, 1932, by Senator Frazier of North Dakota. The measure urges a literal interpretation of the Pact. "Whereas the United States is a signatory to the general pact (or Kellogg pact) signed at Paris August 27, 1928," it asks the Senate, among other things, to recommend to the United States delegates attending the Geneva Disarmament Conference—

that they refuse to concern themselves with the war plans and war preparations of any nation or with such irrelevant matters as budgets, percentages, man power, effectives, gun elevations, or with any other detail of organized murder, the mere discussion of which presupposes the continuation of the war system and the violation of the general pact.

The resolution also asks the Senate to urge the American delegates to "secure the agreement of the Conference" to a "multilateral treaty, which shall be sent by the delegates to their respective governments for approval and ratification." Articles I and II of the treaty proposed in Senator Frazier's resolution and the two articles of the Pact of Paris are identical. The third and final article of the Senator's treaty says:

> Article 3. The high contracting parties pledge themselves in the names of their respective peoples to immediate and complete disarmament, and hereby declare that it shall be a violation of international law for any nation, State, or subdivision thereof, or for any league, group, or association of nations, to take part in any war, offensive or defensive, or to prepare for, declare, or carry on any armed expedition, invasion, or undertaking, or to raise, appropriate, or expend funds for such purposes.

The third article of this resolution, it must be admitted, is a test of sincerity and an unequivocal thrust at national and international hypocrisy. Also, it may do much to buttress the growth of the idea which is gradually breaking down the nationalist viewpoint in favor of a more humanitarian outlook.

Practical support has already been given to a literal interpretation of the General Pact for the Renunciation of War. In a belated five-point proposal initiated on February 2,

1932, by the United States and supported by Great Britain, France and Italy, Japan and China were asked to cease hostilities and "to settle all outstanding controversies . . . in the spirit of the Pact of Paris." Thus, although it must be admitted that this four-power proposal carried no weight with the military caste of Japan, progress was made in that the four great Powers' note actually named the Kellogg Pact instead of merely making a vague reference to it.[119]

In view of this adherence to the Kellogg Pact by the State Department of the United States, there would seem to be an inherent conflict of policy in a government which through its War Department, fosters a "war policies" commission on the one hand, and on the other, through its State Department, sends a note to a foreign power calling its attention to the spirit of the Pact of Paris.

Whatever change occurs in political theory or practice affecting the Pact of Paris, it would seem that Congress, in creating the War Policies Commission, was under the influence of the war-for-defense school.

However, I assume that the United States will not de-

[119] Alluding to the fact that the foreign powers did not take energetic action in support of the Pact of Paris until the Japanese broke "some windows" in the International Settlement during the aerial bombardment of the Chinese Quarter in Shanghai, H. N. Brailsford, the brilliant English journalist—through the mouth of an imagined "Swedish traveler" on his way to the Disarmament Conference at Geneva—said: "The Kellogg Pact was loosely drafted. It ought to be clarified. The signatories might make it clear that they 'renounce war as an instrument of national policy wherever native cities are in close proximity to European settlements.' Justice may wear a bandage on her eyes, but she is not color blind." (*See* Baltimore Sun, Feb. 24, 1932.)

liberately declare a war except for legitimately defensive purposes.

One of the difficulties in using the term "defensive" is that our foreign policy has not been clearly defined. If the Unted States means to protect every dollar abroad, whether it be in a remote town on the Yangtze River or in Mexico, then the term "defensive" has a different connotation. But if President Hoover's October 27, 1931, statement—

> The first necessity of our government is the maintenance of a navy so efficient and strong that, in conjunction with our army, no enemy may ever invade our country. . .
>
> Ours is a force of defense, not offense. To maintain forces less than that strength is to destroy national safety; to maintain greater forces is not only economic injury to our people, but a threat against our neighbors and would be righteous cause for ill-will among them.—

is to be an integral part of our policy, then the word "defensive" has a more literal meaning.[120] Following this interpretation, the assumption that the United States will not deliberately declare a war expect for legitimately defensive purposes is a reasonable one in view of the fact that this country could only be plunged into a purely offensive war or war for purposes of exploitation by those elements of American society who have interests which would suggest such action. Obviously, the people would not tolerate such a war were they aware of its true nature.

120 The dispute between the big and little navy advocates, in a large measure, goes on in its interminable way because of the Government's alternating between a clearly defined imperialistic policy and a strict national defense policy, as outlined in President Hoover's speech.

In nearly all cases of wars of exploitation the difficulty has been the failure to make the people realize their true purpose before they have been stampeded into them by the powerful influence of those who stood to profit by them.

If we wish to eliminate the opportunity for any class to profit from war we must examine certain probabilities inherent in the question of war and peace.

Recent history shows that a major war is accompanied or followed in both victorious and defeated nations by social upheavals tending towards revolution in the latter countries and fundamental changes in the social system in the former.[121] War and social transformation go hand in hand.[122] One may attribute this seeming historical prin-

[121] With the end of the War, the released social energies found form in a world movement for leveling economic and political inequalities. In the defeated countries, it expressed itself in revolutions and near-revolutions. In the victorious countries, it was manifest in demands for reconstruction in which the laboring masses were to have higher economic and political status. The political and social upheaval was carried along by the post-Armistice boom, and by the Bolshevik Revolution which dramatized to the world the idea of the masses coming into power. In the demand for a legal eight-hour day, for workers' control, for industrial councils in Great Britain, for the Plumb Plan in the United States, for national ownership of public utilities, for national economic councils in Germany and France, the pre-War ideas of social ownership and of public regulation, were merged with the incipient idea of planning, thus bringing into focus a newer and more realistic concept of national control and coordination.—Lewis L. Lorwin, one of the leading American authorities on national planning, in an article entitled "The Origins of Economic Planning" in the February 1932 *Survey Graphic.*

[122] An editorial in *Pravda* (reported in a wireless story to the New York *Times* of February 13, 1932) on Maxim Litvinoff's speech to the Disarmament Conference delegates weaves this fact into the Soviet outlook. It said:

The Soviet delegation put the whole question of disarmament in the ciple to the fact that wars aggravate the inequalities between social groups and classes that exist during periods of peace. These inequalities will be more sharply outlined and will be particularly aggravated if our policies during war-time allow the stronger elements of society to take advantage of their strength and position to make either extra or "normal" profits at the expense of the other classes. Therefore, if we desire to avoid the danger of acute social conflict while we are ostensibly or actually engaged in defending ourselves against aggression, we must see to it that our economic policies during war are so shaped as not to result in sharpening the economic inequalities or in provoking class conflict to a condition which may have serious effects.

Aside from this fact, the desire for equalizing the burdens of war is strengthened by the feeling of plain justice that no person and no group in the State should dare to assume the moral responsibility of calling upon others to risk the supreme sacrifice of life unless they themselves submit to the same risk. Unfortunately, it is impossible to mold this moral principle into an active law. In no war can all members of the nation submit to the same sacrifice or assume the same risks. By the very nature of war there

sharpest perspective and however imperialist leaders try to manoeuvre they will not be able to distract the attention of the international proletariat from the points raised by our delegation at Geneva. The imperialist tricks will be exposed and the revolutionary proletariat in all lands will do everything to prevent war and, if it comes, to change the imperialist war into civil war and turn the weapons against its own oppressors.

is an inequality of human risks. We leave aside, therefore, the question of equalizing the burdens of war in that moral sense. It is imperative, however, to consider measures for preventing war from resulting in new as well as greater economic inequalities.

The problem may be formulated in a series of specific questions:

(1) Shall we temporarily suspend the operation of the profit system in war-time?

> Theoretically this could be accomplished either by placing everyone on a fixed salary basis or by declaring that the products of industry not taken by the State for prosecuting war be equally divided among the civilian population. While perhaps morally the most justifiable, this plan would not be practicable or feasible administratively since to assure its reasonable success in war-time too extensive arrangements would have to be made by the government in peace-time. And secondly, preparation in peace-time for a war-time suspension of the profit system would be opposed by the overwhelming majority of business interests as a wedge for an attempt to make this suspension permanent in war and peace.

(2) Since this suspension of the profit system is impracticable and impolitic at the present time, shall we then set a maximum profit for the duration of the war which would be in fixed proportion to the earnings of workers, which profit might be below the level of the so-called "just

compensation" rate, that is, the general profit earnings enjoyed in peace-time?

A control of the absolute or net amount suggests itself because of the certainty that with the increased business of war-time the continuance of the peace-time profit rate will produce larger absolute profits and create new war millionaires. In addition, the impossibility of accurate government supervision of corporation accounts and the various subterfuges by which excess profits taxes and other taxes of this nature can be avoided mean that the government will not be able to recapture such excess profits through any tax medium.

Concerning the constitutional nature of this question, it is well known that the Government under the Fifth Amendment may take private property for public use in war or peace providing "just compensation" is paid. It is not generally understood, however, that the settlement of what constitutes "just compensation" is a judicial function. In the case of United States v. New River Collieries Company, 262 U. S. Reports, 341, which was decided on May 21, 1923, the Supreme Court held: "The ascertainment of compensation is a judicial function, and no power exists in any other department of the government to declare what the compensation shall be or to prescribe any binding rule in that regard."

Thus the inherent powers now vested in the President do not permit him to fix or freeze either a maximum profit or a maximum price in war-time. To give him that power it will be necessary to repeal or modify the "just compensation" clause of the Fifth Amendment. Obviously, any legislation permitting Congress to draft or confiscate property in war-time for public use would have to be supported by such an amendment to the Constitution.

A report made to the Commission by Alexander Holtzoff, Special Assistant to the Attorney-General, Chairman of the Legal Section; George P. Hill, Major, Judge Advocate, United States Army; and Robert A. Lavender, Lieutenant Commander, United States Navy, although it states that it is not rendering a legal opinion on the constitutionality of Mr. Baruch's proposed plan for price-freezing in war-time nevertheless seems to give all the authority necessary for the conclusion that the plan is unconstitutional:

Preliminary Observations in Reference to Mr. Baruch's Plan for Fixing Prices

It is not the purpose of the legal section at this time to render an opinion as to the constitutionality of Mr. Baruch's proposed plan for the fixing of prices during war time. The legal section is engaged in making a complete and exhaustive study of the constitutional powers of the Federal Government in that direction and will submit at a later date the results of its work, accompanied by an expression of views as to the constitutionality of the various plans that may be under consideration by the commission.

The purpose of this memorandum is merely tentatively to suggest for consideration, some problems and queries in connection with the study of the constitutionality of Mr. Baruch's plan. . . .

All discussions of the constitutionality of such a price-fixing scheme during periods of emergency must rest upon the axiom that the Federal Constitution is not suspended during war time. (Ex parte Milligan, 4 Wall. 2)

It is equally well established that the fifth amendment to the Constitution, prohibiting the taking of private property for public use, without fair compensation, is as efficacious in war time as it is in peace time. (United States v. Russell, 13 Wall. 623; United States v. L. Cohen Grocery Co., 255 U. S. 81; United States v. New River Collieries, 262 U. S. 34.)

What constitutes fair compensation is a judicial question and its final determination must be made by the courts. (United States v. New River Collieries, 262 U. S. 341; Seaboard Air Line Railway v. United States, 261 U. S. 299, 304; Monongahela Navigation Co. v. United States, 148 U. S. 319, 327.)

There would seem to be no doubt that the validity of price-fixing methods must be tested by recourse to the fifth amendment, since the fixing of prices, to a certain extent, circumscribes the right of the owner of a piece of property to dispose of it as he chooses, and to that extent may constitute a partial taking of property.

It would seem therefore that any scheme for the regulation of prices which attempts to eliminate an opportunity for a court review of the fairness and justice of the price fixed would be unconstitutional.

The doctrine seems to be firmly established that ordinarily the fixing of prices by legislative or executive fiat is valid only in the case of callings coupled with a public interest, such as common carriers, public utilities, insurance companies, etc. Even then it must be subject to court review.

(Munn v. Illinois, 94 U. S. 113; German Alliance Insurance Company v. Lewis, 233 U. S. 389.). . .

The question arises whether or not to uphold universal price-fixing in war time it will be necessary for the courts to go one step further than they have so far gone, namely, to hold that because of the modern methods of warfare, which involve the Nation as a whole rather than merely its armed forces, the emergency is so widespread and the regulative force of competition so universally restricted as to clothe with public interest all dealings in commodities and services, whether for public or private consumption, whether at wholesale or retail. Whether or not that proposition can be sustained is, in its ultimate analysis, the question to be answered.

Again, it is necessary to determine to what extent, if any, some form of court review would be regarded as an indispensable prerequisite to the validity of any price-fixing plan.

As stated above, the legal section is not at this time ready to express any final or definite views as to the constitutionality of Mr. Baruch's scheme. This is a matter which is now being studied.

The foregoing observations were made to outline some of the problems which are being considered.[123]

It is interesting to note that this constitutional point was discussed by President Hoover in 1924 when, as Secretary of Commerce, he addressed a letter to Representative John J. McSwain during the hearings before the House Committee on Military Affairs, in which he not only approved legalizing "a blanket authority to the President to fix prices, wages, transportation charges,

[123] War Policies Commission Hearings, pages 839–41.

compensation, embargoes on imports and exports," but also the authority to "suspend habeas corpus." The letter, in part, said:

> . . . I would also suggest that from a legal point of view a general clause should be added to the bill giving a blanket authority to the President to fix prices, wages, transportation charges, compensations, embargoes on imports and exports; to exercise the war powers of requisition under circumstances that 75 per cent of the estimated value may be paid and the balance determined by the courts in case of disagreement; suspend habeas corpus, and generally complete an absolute authority in all ramifications over the whole civilian life with the provision that he may delegate these authorities through these various agencies. . .[124]

(3) If we desire to eliminate profits made during war-time and thus lessen the danger of the consequent social upheaval, and to work out an economic program which would tend to make war less likely, is it not clear that we are more likely to do so by undertaking to develop a progressive national economy through scientific planning? Since whatever social injustices exist in peace-time are aggravated by war is it not clear that we can more readily overcome them under peace-time conditions, and in so doing perform a twofold function by also making war less likely?

In introducing his suggestion for action which would lead towards a "planned national economy" Professor

[124] Tentative Draft for Consideration by Members of the Commission Created by Public Resolution No. 98, 71st Cong., pages 47–48. This letter is also printed in the hearings before the Committee on Military Affairs on "Universal Mobilization for War Purposes," *op. cit.*, page 194.

Robert Morss Lovett referred to the necessity for a body whose function would be the regulation of production and distribution, the direction of capital investments, the organization of the labor market, and other necessary cognate endeavors. Concerning the relation of this type of economy to war and peace, he said to the Commission:

> The direction and control of industry in the interest of the general welfare is becoming more and more necessary in time of peace as it is in time of war. It would be, I believe, unfortunate to give plans in this direction the hall mark of war. In fact, a planned national economy conduces to the chief object of the resolution under which we are here—to promote peace. A century ago Cobden and the English free traders thought they had found a solvent for war in free trade. They were wrong. They did not foresee the export of capital, the struggle for markets, the various economic developments which have proved fruitful occasions of war. But surely they were on the right track when they argued that the causes of war must give way to concerted interests in prosperity, which, they were also right in arguing, must be a general condition in which the whole world participates. More than ever is it clear to-day that no nation lives to itself alone—that if one member suffers, the others suffer with it.[125]

As long as we admit war into the social picture, this form of planning, if realized, would tend to make the transition stage between war and peace less difficult for the reason that new agencies will not have to be created

[125] War Policies Commission Hearings, pages 538–39.

precipitately. Thus a national economic planning board could easily function as a war-time planning board. It is almost of equal importance that such a program would save the tax-payers enormous sums since the country would not be obliged to pay the usual huge premium for inexperience in mobilizing and coordinating the country's economic resources.

"National planning," as Professor Lovett informed the Commission, must also "take account of international relations." He said:

> Its ultimate end is the utilization of the resources of the entire world in the most efficient manner. Rationalization of foreign trade, apportionment of raw materials, direction of investments in foreign countries all are means to this end. As national planning develops in other countries, and certain of them are already in advance of the United States in this matter, mutual arrangements will be easier to achieve. With this closer weaving of the economic fabric of human society, the relations of nations with one another will tend to become more stable, their interests more reciprocal, the dislocation of war more unthinkable.[126]

To avoid mistakes which may discredit this planned national economy at the outset and which might very well cause some of the needless expense it is designed to avoid, it is necessary to determine what existing governmental agencies there are whose organization and experience could be utilized towards furthering such a planning program. Besides correlating official statistical data such a determina-

[126] *Ibid.*, page 539.

tion will prevent the duplication of already existing governmental machinery. If followed by a very careful survey of the country's resources there is every reason to believe that we will obtain the information necessary to lay the foundation for a rational national economy.[127]

Economic revolution is inevitable. In the light of present worldwide conditions such a statement is nearly a truism. The only question is—what will be its nature?

Undue postponement of a rational national economy may mean that the revolution will be a violent instead of a peaceful one—either as the result of a war with a foreign power in the course of which existing social inequalities would be sharply aggravated or by civil war induced mainly by intolerable domestic conditions.

Thus it would seem that those in control of our economic order would be wiser to make sincere efforts to inject more

[127] It will be readily appreciated that the definition and development of national planning is not the province of this book. However, the following definition given by Lewis L. Lorwin in the March 1932 *Survey Graphic*, is instructive and helpful to those interested in the subject:

> A planned economy may, in general terms, be defined as a scheme of economic organization in which individual and separate plants, enterprises, and industries are treated as coordinated units of one single system for the purpose of utilizing all available resources to achieve the maximum satisfaction of the people's needs within a given time. The essential features are: the interdependence of all productive units, the adjustment of a progressively growing productive mechanism with a progressively rising standard of living, and the existence of some unifying center to direct the system consciously towards these nationally recognized objectives.

At this writing Senator La Follette has announced the introduction of a bill which would establish a National Economic Council with specific powers for fact finding and recommendation.

than a semblance of reason and justice in it rather than to use their power and ingenuity to secure the continuance of profits in war-time, a contingency which may end by wiping out both their lives and their property.

Their failure to use the opportunity presented to them by the War Policies Commission may make the relation between death and profits uncomfortably close.